Modern Poems for the Commonwealth

Edited by Maurice Wollman
in 'Harrap's English Classics'
TWENTIETH-CENTURY NARRATIVE POEMS
TEN TWENTIETH-CENTURY POETS
TEN CONTEMPORARY POETS

Edited by Maurice Wollman and Kathleen B. Parker
in 'Harrap's Modern English Series'
THE HARRAP BOOK OF MODERN VERSE

Edited by Maurice Wollman and Dorothy M. Hurst
in 'Harrap's Modern English Series'
HARRAP'S JUNIOR BOOK OF MODERN VERSE

Edited by Maurice Wollman and David Grugeon
HAPPENINGS

---

by John Spencer in 'Harrap's World Ahead Series'
WORKERS FOR HUMANITY

MODERN POEMS

for the

COMMONWEALTH

Selected and Edited by

MAURICE WOLLMAN M.A.
The Perse School, Cambridge

and

JOHN SPENCER M.A. (Oxon.)
Senior Lecturer in Contemporary English
The University of Leeds

GEORGE G. HARRAP & CO. LTD
London · Toronto · Wellington · Sydney

First published in Great Britain 1966
by GEORGE G. HARRAP & CO. LTD
182 High Holborn, London, W.C.1

Composed in Monotype Perpetua and printed by
Western Printing Services Ltd, Bristol
Made in Great Britain

Preface

THE poems in this collection were all written in this century, most of them by poets still living. They show the modern poet looking at our world, at the present of our century in relation to the past or the future. They demonstrate that the poet's vision can embrace all things, places, times and peoples. These poems show too that, even when it is not cast in traditional metrical moulds, poetry is still poetry.

The English language today is used by writers all over the world, and poets are writing English verse in all the five continents. It is therefore proper that this collection of modern poems should contain some of the work of poets from the Americas, from Africa, Asia, Australia, and New Zealand, as well as from the British Isles. Less than ever before can it be claimed that English poetry is poetry written by Englishmen. The English poetic tradition has now taken root in many places across the globe, and is being enriched as a result.

Modern poetry is sometimes held to be obscure. This may be because those who judge it to be so are misled by the modern poet's readiness to discard older metrical forms; or by his insistence on writing about what he sees and feels in a new twentieth-century way; or, perhaps more significantly, by the poet's need to portray with integrity his vision of a world grown more complex and, at the same time, more uncertain of itself. That these characteristics of modern poetry have not in fact led to obscurity—indeed, are not such revolutionary features as has sometimes been supposed—the reader of this book may test for himself.

Nevertheless, the language through which the poet conveys his vision is not always straightforward or simple. Sometimes the poet must bend or compress the language to match his purposes. He may use fragments of archaic language, to produce an echo of strangeness or remoteness; he may utilize colloquial language, dialect terms, or even slang, for intimacy or comic effect; he will often attempt, by means of unusual metaphors, by linking words not commonly associated, to give shocks of vividness, surprise, or irony.

Some assistance in the matter of language and references or background is given in the Notes, wherever it seemed that the reader's dictionary alone would not help. But the Editors have deliberately avoided offering 'interpretations' of any of the poems, believing that thus to interpose themselves between poet and reader would be doing a disservice to both.

M.W., J.S.

Index of Authors

Law Like Love

W. H. AUDEN

LAW, say the gardeners, is the sun,
Law is the one
All gardeners obey
To-morrow, yesterday, to-day.

Law is the wisdom of the old
The impotent grandfathers shrilly scold;
The grandchildren put out a treble tongue,
Law is the senses of the young.

Law, says the priest with a priestly look,
Expounding to an unpriestly people,
Law is the words in my priestly book,
Law is my pulpit and my steeple.

Law, says the judge as he looks down his nose,
Speaking clearly and most severely,
Law is as I've told you before,
Law is as you know I suppose,
Law is but let me explain it once more,
Law is the Law.

Yet law-abiding scholars write;
Law is neither wrong nor right,
Law is only crimes
Punished by places and by times,
Law is the clothes men wear
Anytime, anywhere,
Law is Good-morning and Good-night.

Others say, Law is our Fate;
Others say, Law is our State;
Others say, others say
Law is no more
Law has gone away.

And always the loud angry crowd
Very angry and very loud
Law is We,
And always the soft idiot softly Me.

If we, dear, know we know no more
Than they about the law,
If I no more than you
Know what we should and should not do
Except that all agree
Gladly or miserably
That the law is
And that all know this,
If therefore thinking it absurd
To identify Law with some other word,
Unlike so many men
I cannot say Law is again,
No more than they can we suppress
The universal wish to guess
Or slip out of our own position
Into an unconcerned condition.

Although I can at least confine
Your vanity and mine
To stating timidly
A timid similarity,
We shall boast anyway:
Like love I say.

Like love we don't know where or why
Like love we can't compel or fly
Like love we often weep
Like love we seldom keep.

The Will

JOHN MASEFIELD

BY Will, Man dared in den and heath
The dagger-claws and sabre-teeth
And brought their savageries beneath.

By Will, he beat the flint to fire
And burned the jungle in his ire
And lit the dark to his desire.

By Will, his spirit tamed the force
Of the wild bull and the wild horse
And the wild river in her course.

By Will, he quarried and made bright
Stone spires lifting into light
With visions of the infinite.

By Will, he made him eyes to see
The Death that Kills in secrecy
From fly and louse and gnat and flea.

By Will, he made him slaves with hands
That without word do his commands
In air, in oceans and in lands.

Earth, water, air and brute and fool,
And crazy rebel against rule
By Will, he made each one his tool.

And shall he not, by Will, attack,
The country's shame, the peoples' lack,
The rags upon the nation's back?

The blots upon the nation's mind
The ignorance that makes us blind
The hate, that shuts us from our Kind?

Surely, by Will, he will blow clear
His trumpets that all ears shall hear,
And helping angels shall sweep near,

And the banners of the soul advance,
Up, out of hate and ignorance,
Into a new inheritance.

Is

PATRICK KAVANAGH

THE important thing is not
To imagine one ought
Have something to say,
A raison d'être, a plot for the play.
The only true teaching
Subsists in watching
Things moving or just colour
Without comment from the scholar.
To look on is enough
In the business of love.
Casually remark
On a deer running in a park;
Mention water again
Always virginal,
Always original,
It washes out Original Sin.
Name for the future
The everydays of nature
And without being analytic

Create a great epic.
Girls in red blouses,
Steps up to houses,
Sunlight round gables,
Gossip's young fables,
The life of a street.
O wealthy me! O happy state!
With an inexhaustible theme
I'll die in harness,
I'll die in harness with my scheme.

Craftsmen

GEOFFREY JOHNSON

MY ancestors as far as records go
Were metal founders, men of sturdy frame
Who proved their manhood by the furnace glow
And took their wages, with no thought of fame.

Anonymous works they wrung from stubborn ore
Are shining still about the world, and bear
As sure as signatures of men no more
Their pride of craftsmanship and character.

I, weaker-sinewed, tried in other fire,
Toil with the worse recalcitrance of words.
I too, though wilding from the stock, aspire
To sublimate in beauty scraps and sherds.

Enough for, known or unknown, if I
Can shape to endure for half as long a spell
And sometimes to delight a passer-by
One tale or lyric flawless as a bell.

Autobiography

A CHILD, the soft-pawed sky held up my kites.
Tumultuous images rose from the mud.
My eyes like fish flickered through sunken lights
Under the poems dancing in my blood.
And from this great, this all-gate-breaking flood,
My thoughts like pincers lifted tastes and sights.
My heart delved down to love, knowledge of God,
Waited the king in sandals on the heights.

But even then I was as cold as stone,
Sinking among the ripples of the crowd,
And now all my desire is to atone
For an unfriendly springtime, webbed in cloud.
I remember my grandmother, crescent-browed,
Falling from Time, leaf-light, too much alone:
And my grandfather, who was small and proud.
Tumult of images, where have you gone?

The ageing chemist in his drawing-room, terse,
Gentle: the sea like soapsuds in the night,
Seen from a ship: the moon, leprous, inverse,
Rising: the girl at Hanoi with her white
Hands and dog's eyes, dripping with amber light:
Have these things shaped me for the craft of verse?
Do they remain, giving a sad insight?
And have I changed for better or for worse?

I have grown up, I think, to live alone,
To keep my old illusions, sometimes dream

[16]

Glumly that I am unloved and forlorn,
Run away from strangers, often seem
Unreal to myself in the pulpy warmth of a sunbeam.
I have grown up, hand on the primal bone,
Making the poem, taking the word from the stream,
Fighting the sand for speech, fighting the stone.

Lives

HENRY REED

YOU cannot cage a field.
    You cannot wire it, as you wire a summer's roses
To sell in towns; you cannot cage it
Or kill it utterly. All you can do is to force
Year after year from the stream to the cold woods
The heavy glitter of wheat, till its body tires
And the yield grows weaker and dies. But the field never
    dies,
Though you build on it, burn it black, or domicile
A thousand prisoners upon its empty features.
You cannot kill a field. A field will reach
Right under the streams to touch the limbs of its brothers.

But you can cage the woods.
You can throw up fences, as round a recalcitrant heart
Spring up remonstrances. You can always cage the woods,
Hold them completely. Confine them to hill or valley,
You can alter their face, their shape; uprooting their outer
    saplings
You can even alter their wants, and their smallest longings
Press to your own desires. The woods succumb
To the paths made through their life, withdraw the trees,
Betake themselves where you tell them, and acquiesce.

The woods retreat; their protest of leaves whirls
Pitifully to the cooling heavens, like dead or dying prayers.

But what can you do with a stream?
You can widen it here, or deepen it there, but even
If you alter its course entirely it gives the impression
That this is what it always wanted. Moorhens return
To nest or hide in the reeds which quickly grow up there,
The fishes breed in it, stone settles on to stone.
The stream announces its places where the water will
   bubble
Daily and unconcerned, contentedly ruffling and scuffling
With the drifting sky or the leaf. Whatever you do,
A stream has rights, for a stream is always water;
To cross it you have to bridge it; and it will not flow uphill.

Choosing a Mast

ROY CAMPBELL

THIS mast, new-shaved, through whom I rive the ropes,
   Says she was once an oread of the slopes,
Graceful and tall upon the rocky highlands,
A slender tree as vertical as noon,
And her low voice was lovely as the silence
Through which a fountain whistles to the moon,
Who now of the white spray must take the veil
And, for her songs, the thunder of the sail.

I chose her for her fragrance, when the spring
With sweetest resins swelled her fourteenth ring
And with live amber welded her young thews:
I chose her for the glory of the Muse,
Smoother of forms, that her hard-knotted grain,

Grazed by the chisel, shaven by the plane,
Might from the steel as cool a burnish take
As from the bladed moon a windless lake.

I chose her for her eagerness of flight
Where she stood tiptoe on the rocky height
Lifted by her own perfume to the sun,
While through her rustling plumes with eager sound
Her eagle spirit, with the gale at one,
Spreading wide pinions, would have spurned the ground
And her own sleeping shadow, had they not
With thymy fragrance charmed her to the spot.

Lover of song, I chose this mountain pine
Not only for the straightness of her spine
But for her songs: for there she loved to sing
Through a long noon's repose of wave and wing,
The fluvial swirling of her scented hair
Sole rill of song in all that windless air,
And her slim form the naiad of the stream
Afloat upon the languor of its theme;

And for the soldier's fare on which she fed:
Her wine the azure, and the snow her bread;
And for her stormy watches on the height,
For only out of solitude or strife
Are born the sons of valour and delight;
And lastly for her rich exulting life
That with the wind stopped not its singing breath
But carolled on, the louder for its death.

Under a pine, when summer days were deep,
We loved the most to lie in love or sleep:
And when in long hexameters the west
Rolled his grey surge, the forest for his lyre,
It was the pines that sang us to our rest,
Loud in the wind and fragrant in the fire,
With legioned voices swelling all night long,
From Pelion to Provence, their storm of song.

It was the pines that fanned us in the heat,
The pines, that cheered us in the time of sleet,
For which sweet gifts I set one dryad free;
No longer to the wind a rooted foe,
This nymph shall wander where she longs to be
And with the blue north wind arise and go,
A silver huntress with the moon to run
And fly through rainbows with the rising sun;

And when to pasture in the glittering shoals
The guardian mistral drives his thundering foals,
And when like Tartar horsemen racing free
We ride the snorting fillies of the sea,
My pine shall be the archer of the gale
While on the bending willow curves the sail
From whose great bow the long keel shooting home
Shall fly, the feathered arrow of the foam.

To Walk on Hills

ROBERT GRAVES

TO walk on hills is to employ legs
As porters of the head and heart
Jointly adventuring towards
Perhaps true equanimity.

To walk on hills is to see sights
And hear sounds unfamiliar.
When in wind the pine-tree roars,
When crags with bleatings echo,
When water foams below the fall,
Heart records that journey
As memorable indeed;
Head reserves opinion,
Confused by the wind.

A view of three shires and the sea!
Seldom so much at once appears
Of the coloured world, says heart.
Head is glum, says nothing.

Legs become weary, halting
To sprawl in a rock's shelter,
While the sun drowsily blinks
On head at last brought low—
This giddied passenger of legs
That has no word to utter.

Heart does double duty,
As heart, and as head,
With portentous trifling.
A castle, on its crag perched,
Across the miles between is viewed
With awe as across years.

Now a daisy pleases,
Pleases and astounds, even,
That on a garden lawn could blow
All summer long with no esteem.

And the buzzard's cruel poise,
And the plover's misery,
And the important beetle's
Blue-green-shiny back. . . .

To walk on hills is to employ legs
To march away and lose the day.
Confess, have you known shepherds?
And are they not a witless race,
Prone to quaint visions?
Not thus from solitude
(Solitude sobers only)
But from long hilltop striding.

Birds

JUDITH WRIGHT

WHATEVER the bird is, is perfect in the bird.
  Weapon kestrel hard as a blade's curve,
thrush round as a mother or a full drop of water,
fruit-green parrot wise in his shrieking swerve—
all are what bird is and do not reach beyond bird.

Whatever the bird does is right for the bird to do—
cruel kestrel dividing in his hunger the sky,
thrush in the trembling dew beginning to sing,
parrot clinging and quarrelling and veiling his queer eye—
all these are as birds are and good for birds to do.

But I am torn and beleaguered by my own people.
The blood that feeds my heart is the blood they gave me,
and my heart is the house where they gather and fight
    for dominion—
all different, all with a wish and a will to save me,
to turn me into the ways of other people.

If I could leave their battleground for the forest of a bird
I could melt the past, the present and the future in one
and find the words that lie behind all these languages.
Then I could fuse my passions into one clear stone
and be simple to myself as the bird is to the bird.

The Exposed Nest

ROBERT FROST

YOU were forever finding some new play.
So when I saw you down on hands and knees
In the meadow, busy with the new-cut hay,
Trying, I thought, to set it up on end,
I went to show you how to make it stay,
If that was your idea, against the breeze,
And, if you asked me, even help pretend
To make it root again and grow afresh.
But 'twas no make-believe with you today,
Nor was the grass itself your real concern,
Though I found your hand full of wilted fern,
Steel-bright June-grass, and blackening heads of clover.
'Twas a nest full of young birds on the ground
The cutter-bar had just gone champing over
(Miraculously without tasting flesh)
And left defenceless to the heat and light.
You wanted to restore them to their right
Of something interposed between their sight
And too much world at once—could means be found.
The way the nest-full every time we stirred
Stood up to us as to a mother-bird
Whose coming home has been too long deferred,
Made me ask would the mother-bird return
And care for them in such a change of scene
And might our meddling make her more afraid.
That was a thing we could not wait to learn.
We saw the risk we took in doing good,
But dared not spare to do the best we could
Though harm should come of it; so built the screen

You had begun, and gave them back their shade.
All this to prove we cared. Why is there then
No more to tell? We turned to other things.
I haven't any memory—have you?—
Of ever coming to the place again
To see if the birds lived the first night through,
And so at last to learn to use their wings.

Hawk Roosting

TED HUGHES

I SIT in the top of the wood, my eyes closed.
Inaction, no falsifying dream
Between my hooked head and hooked feet:
Or in sleep rehearse perfect kills and eat.

The convenience of the high trees!
The air's buoyancy and the sun's ray
Are of advantage to me;
And the earth's face upward for my inspection.

My feet are locked upon the rough bark.
It took the whole of Creation
To produce my foot, my each feather:
Now I hold Creation in my foot

Or fly up, and revolve it all slowly—
I kill where I please because it is all mine.
There is no sophistry in my body:
My manners are tearing off heads—

The allotment of death.
For the one path of my flight is direct
Through the bones of the living.
No arguments assert my right:

The sun is behind me.
Nothing has changed since I began.
My eye has permitted no change.
I am going to keep things like this.

The Gull

MICHAEL THWAITES

RIDING the wind, in planetary sweep
The gull wheels on the radius of a wing;
Ocean and air, concourse of height and deep,
Acclaim the exultant orbit of their king.

Precise he lands, defter than any dancer,
Red legs, red eye, white body whiter than foam;
No loveliest yacht so light to lean and answer,
No soul so white in its celestial home.

O Attic joy, O grace made visible,
Beauty and power embodied into bird!
Malice, or truth—which is it pricks your spell
With sarcasm of the loathsome and absurd?

Those lacquered feathers, sleek to wind and wave,
Or downy to the softly-fingering breeze,
Are an infested jungle, a living grave,
The haunt of lice, mites, parasites, and fleas.

Filth feeds that savage beauty; when head, beak, eyes
Plunge in the putrid whale, or, harsh as sin,
Are stretched agape, with cannibalistic cries,
To tear the wounded body of his kin.

O beauty born of death, to death returning,
You are our Middle Earth, nor Heaven nor Hell;
You are ourselves, our turning globe still turning,
The fractured light in which we have to dwell.

Here truth is ever tangent. Therefore, gull,
Gorged with the stinking offal that you eat,
Rise in the light, infested, beautiful,
In fragmentary loveliness complete.

Tree Party

LOUIS MACNEICE

YOUR health, Master Willow. Contrive me a bat
To strike a red ball; apart from that
In the last resort I must hang my harp on you.

Your health, Master Oak. You emblem of strength,
Why must your doings be done at such length?
Beware lest the ironclad ages catch up with you.

Your health, Master Blackthorn. Be live and be quick,
Provide the black priest with a big black stick
That his ignorant flock may go straight for the fear
of you.

Your health, Master Palm. If you brew us some toddy
To deliver us out of by means of the body,
We will burn all our bridges and rickshaws in praise
of you.

Your health, Master Pine. Though sailing be past
Let you fly your own colours upon your own mast
And rig us a crow's nest to keep a look out from you.

Your health, Master Elm. Of giants arboreal
Poets have found you the most immemorial
And yet the big winds may discover the fault in you.

Your health, Master Hazel. On Hallowe'en
Your nuts are to gather but not to be seen
Are the twittering ghosts that perforce are alive in you.

Your health, Master Holly. Of all the trees
That decorate parlour walls you please
Yet who would have thought you had so much blood
    in you?

Your health, Master Apple. Your topmost bough
Entices us to come climbing now
For all that old rumour there might be a snake in you.

Your health, Master Redwood. The record is yours
For the girth that astounds, the sap that endures,
But where are the creatures that once came to nest
    in you?

Your health, Master Banyan, but do not get drunk
Or you may not distinguish your limbs from your trunk
And the sense of Above and Below will be lost on you.

Your health, Master Bo-Tree. If Buddha should come
Yet again, yet again make your branches keep mum
That his words yet again may drop honey by leave
    of you.

Your health, Master Yew. My bones are few
And I fully admit my rent is due,
But do not be vexed, I will postdate a cheque for you.

First Sight

PHILIP LARKIN

LAMBS that learn to walk in snow
When their bleating clouds the air
Meet a vast unwelcome, know
Nothing but a sunless glare.
Newly stumbling to and fro
All they find, outside the fold,
Is a wretched width of cold.

As they wait beside the ewe,
Her fleeces wetly caked, there lies
Hidden round them, waiting too,
Earth's immeasurable surprise.
They could not grasp it if they knew,
What so soon will wake and grow
Utterly unlike the snow.

The Red Squirrel

GEOFFREY JOHNSON

THE small red squirrel every morning toes
The dew-strung tightrope of my fence's wire,
Climbs up the bird-trough with the speed of fire,
Squats in its hold of natural fir-bark, stows

Good bread inside him, drops where instinct knows
  Thick rhododendrons hide the nesting choir,
    Sucks a few eggs, then rounds the meal with hire
And emptying of their drinking bowl. He goes.

All watchfulness burns in his eye's wet bead
  That holds the heathery wild from which he came;
    Yet unaware of joy or pain he wrought
As of the havoc hawking for his breed;
  Near as my finger, yet remote as flame
    Of the north star; elusive as a thought.

The Greater Cats

V. SACKVILLE-WEST

THE greater cats with golden eyes
  Stare out between the bars.
Deserts are theirs, and different skies,
  And night with different stars.
They prowl the aromatic hill,
And mate as fiercely as they kill,
And hold the freedom of their will
To roam, to live, to drink their fill;
  But this beyond their wit know I:
Man loves a little, and for long shall die.

  Their kind across the desert range
  Where tulips spring from stones,
  Not knowing they will suffer change
  Or vultures pick their bones.
  Their strength's eternal in their sight,
  They rule the terror of the night,
  They overtake the deer in flight,
  And in their arrogance they smite:

But I am sage, if they are strong:
Man's love is transient as his death is long.

Yet oh what powers to deceive!
My wit is turned to faith,
And at this moment I believe
In love, and scout at death.
I came from nowhere, and shall be
Strong, steadfast, swift, eternally:
I am a lion, a stone, a tree,
And as the Polar star in me
Is fixed my constant heart on thee.
Ah, may I stay forever blind
With lions, tigers, leopards, and their kind.

The Dead Crab

ANDREW YOUNG

A ROSY shield upon its back,
  That not the hardest storm could crack,
From whose sharp edge projected out
Black pin-point eyes staring about;
Beneath, the well-knit cote-armure
That gave to its weak belly power;
The clustered legs with plated joints
That ended in stiletto points;
The claws like mouths it held outside:—
I cannot think this creature died
By storm or fish or sea-fowl harmed
Walking the sea so heavily armed;
Or does it make for death to be
Oneself a living armoury?

Baby Tortoise

D. H. LAWRENCE

YOU know what it is to be born alone,
Baby tortoise!

The first day to heave your feet little by little from the shell,
Not yet awake,
And remain lapsed on earth,
Not quite alive.

A tiny, fragile, half-animate bean.

To open your tiny beak-mouth, that looks as if it would never
open,
Like some iron door;
To lift the upper hawk-beak from the lower base
And reach your skinny little neck
And take your first bite at some dim bit of herbage,
Alone, small insect,
Tiny bright-eye,
Slow one.

To take your first solitary bite
And move on your slow, solitary hunt.
Your bright, dark little eye,
Your eye of a dark disturbed night,
Under its slow lid, tiny baby tortoise,
So indomitable.

No one ever heard you complain.

You draw your head forward, slowly, from your little wimple
And set forward, slow-dragging, on your four-pinned toes,
Rowing slowly forward.
Whither away, small bird?
Rather like a baby working its limbs,
Except that you make slow, ageless progress
And a baby makes none.

The touch of sun excites you,
And the long ages, and the lingering chill
Make you pause to yawn,
Opening your impervious mouth,
Suddenly beak-shaped, and very wide, like some suddenly gaping
    pincers;
Soft red tongue, and hard thin gums,
Then close the wedge of your little mountain front,
Your face, baby tortoise.

Do you wonder at the world, as slowly you turn your head in its
    wimple
And look with laconic, black eyes?
Or is sleep coming over you again,
The non-life?

You are so hard to wake.

Are you able to wonder?
Or is it just your indomitable will and pride of the first life
Looking round
And slowly pitching itself against the inertia
Which had seemed invincible?

The vast inanimate,
And the fine brilliance of your so tiny eye,
Challenger.

Nay, tiny shell-bird,
What a huge vast inanimate it is, that you must row against,
What an incalculable inertia.

Challenger,
Little Ulysses, fore-runner,
No bigger than my thumb-nail,
Buon viaggio.

All animate creation on your shoulder,
Set forth, little Titan, under your battle-shield.

The ponderous, preponderate,
Inanimate universe;
And you are slowly moving, pioneer, you alone.

How vivid your travelling seems now, in the troubled sunshine,
Stoic, Ulyssean atom;
Suddenly hasty, reckless, on high toes.

Voiceless little bird,
Resting your head half out of your wimple
In the slow dignity of your eternal pause.
Alone, with no sense of being alone,
And hence six times more solitary;
Fulfilled of the slow passion of pitching through immemorial
    ages
Your little round house in the midst of chaos.

Over the garden earth,
Small bird,
Over the edge of all things.

Traveller,
With your tail tucked a little on one side
Like a gentleman in a long-skirted coat.

All life carried on your shoulder,
Invincible fore-runner.

Elephant

N. H. BRETTELL

SLOWLY the great head turned,
And the late sunlight slept on massive flanks
Like the still slabs of riven krants,
Immovable, and nonchalantly bearing
The burden of the old enormous lies,
The load of legendary centuries,
The mighty turtle and the seas of milk
On which the old World swam;
And slowly folded back the fluted ears
Like pterodactyl's wings drooping to roost.

Slowly the great limbs moved:
The monstrous pistons in the wrinkled sheath,
Unflurried and unhesitating, lift
The huge façade across the afternoon:
Like a great engine, headed north,
With the deliberation of the six-foot wheels
Slides from the vaulted terminus
Down miles of metals through a continent.
Behemoth, baron, lord,
—In trigger-fingered world, one creature left unscathed;
Away from us, over the burnt earth, under the forest branches,
Casually stripping the green crown from a tree,
Going oblivious, the invulnerable beast.

The Giraffes

ROY FULLER

I THINK before they saw me the giraffes
  Were watching me. Over the golden grass,
The bush and ragged open tree of thorn,
From a grotesque height, under their lightish horns,
Their eyes were fixed on mine as I approached them.
The hills behind descended steeply: iron-
Coloured outcroppings of rock half covered by
Dull green and sepia vegetation, dry
And sunlit: and above, the piercing blue
Where clouds like islands lay or like swans flew.

Seen from those hills the scrubby plain is like
A large-scale map whose features have a look
Half menacing, half familiar, and across
Its brightness arms of shadow ceaselessly
Revolve. Like small forked twigs or insects move
Giraffes, upon the great map where they live.

When I went nearer, their long bovine tails
Flicked loosely, and deliberately they turned,
An undulation of dappled grey and brown,
And stood in profile with those curious planes
Of neck and sloping haunches. Just as when,
Quite motionless, they watched I never thought
Them moved by fear, a wish to be a tree,
So as they put more ground between us I
Saw evidence that these were animals
With no desire for intercourse, or no
Capacity.
            Above the falling sun,

Like visible winds the clouds are streaked and spun,
And cold and dark now bring the image of
Those creatures walking without pain or love.

Giraffes

PHOEBE HESKETH

BEYOND the brassy sun-stare where each shade
Crouches beneath its substance at mid-noon,
The tall giraffes are gathered in a glade
Grazing the green fruit of the midday moon.
Patched with sienna shadows of the jungle,
In pencil-slender attitudes they stand;
Grotesque in camouflage, each curve and angle
Is merged into the backcloth of the land.

These circus creatures of a poet's dreaming
Whose destiny on silent strings is spun,
Are patterned in designs of nature's scheming
To move through dappled woods and dun.
Strange genesis in which the substance seeming
The shadow, is the secret of the sun!

Stanley meets Mutesa

DAVID RUBADIRI

SUCH a time of it they had;
The heat of the day
The chill of the night
And the mosquitoes that followed.

Such was the time and
They bound for a kingdom.

The thin weary line of carriers
With tattered dirty rags to cover their backs;
The battered bulky chests
That kept on falling off their shaven heads.
Their tempers high and hot
The sun fierce and scorching
With it rose their spirits
With its fall their hopes
As each day sweated their bodies dry and
Flies clung in clumps on their sweat-scented backs.
Such was the march
And the hot season just breaking.

Each day a weary pony dropped,
Left for the vultures on the plains;
Each afternoon a human skeleton collapsed,
Left for the Masai on the plains;
But the march trudged on
Its Khaki leader in front
He the spirit that inspired.
He the light of hope.

Then came the afternoon of a hungry march,
A hot and hungry march it was;
The Nile and the Nyanza
Lay like two twins
Azure across the green countryside.
The march leapt on chaunting
Like young gazelles to a water hole.
Hearts beat faster
Loads felt lighter
As the cool water lapt their sore soft feet.
No more the dread of hungry hyenas
But only tales of valour when
At Mutesa's court fires are lit.

No more the burning heat of the day
But song, laughter and dance.

The village looks on behind banana groves,
Children peer behind reed fences.
Such was the welcome
No singing women to chaunt a welcome
Or drums to greet the white ambassador;
Only a few silent nods from aged faces
And one rumbling drum roll
To summon Mutesa's court to parley
For the country was not sure.

The gate of reeds is flung open,
There is silence
But only a moment's silence—
A silence of assessment.
The tall black king steps forward,
He towers over the thin bearded white man
Then grabbing his lean white hand
Manages to whisper
'Mtu Mweupe karibu'
White man you are welcome.
The gate of polished reed closes behind them
And the west is let in.

Piano and Drums

GABRIEL OKARA

WHEN at break of day at a riverside
I hear jungle drums telegraphing
the mystic rhythm, urgent, raw
like bleeding flesh, speaking of
primal youth and the beginning,

I see the panther ready to pounce,
the leopard snarling about to leap
and the hunters crouch with spears poised;

And my blood ripples, turns torrent,
topples the years and at once I'm
in my mother's lap a suckling;
at once I'm walking simple
paths with no innovations,
rugged, fashioned with the naked
warmth of hurrying feet and groping hearts
in green leaves and wild flowers pulsing.

Then I hear a wailing piano
solo speaking of complex ways
in tear-furrowed concerto;
of far-away lands
and new horizons with
coaxing diminuendo, counterpoint,
crescendo. But lost in the labyrinth
of its complexities, it ends in the middle
of a phrase at a daggerpoint.

And I lost in the morning mist
of an age at a riverside keep
wandering in the mystic rhythm
of jungle drums and the concerto.

The Sea eats the Land at Home

GEORGE AWOONOR-WILLIAMS

AT home the sea is in the town,
Running in and out of the cooking places,
Collecting the firewood from the hearths
And sending it back at night;
The sea eats the land at home.
It came one day at the dead of night,
Destroying the cement walls,
And carried away the fowls,
The cooking-pots and the ladles,
The sea eats the land at home;
It is a sad thing to hear the wails,
And the mourning shouts of the women,
Calling on all the gods they worship,
To protect them from the angry sea.
Aku stood outside where her cooking-pot stood,
With her two children shivering from the cold,
Her hands on her breast,
Weeping mournfully.
Her ancestors have neglected her,
Her gods have deserted her,
It was a cold Sunday morning,
The storm was raging,
Goats and fowls were struggling in the water,
The angry water of the cruel sea;
The lap-lapping of the bark water at the shore,
And above the sobs and the deep and low moans,
Was the eternal hum of the living sea.
It has taken away their belongings
Adena has lost the trinkets which

Were her dowry and her joy,
In the sea that eats the land at home,
Eats the whole land at home.

The Difficult Land

EDWIN MUIR

THIS is a difficult land. Here things miscarry
Whether we care, or do not care enough.
The grain may pine, the harlot weed grow haughty,
Sun, rain, and frost alike conspire against us:
You'd think there was malice in the very air.
And the spring floods and summer droughts: our fields
Mile after mile of soft and useless dust.
On dull delusive days presaging rain
We yoke the oxen, go out harrowing,
Walk in the middle of an ochre cloud,
Dust rising before us and falling again behind us,
Slowly and gently settling where it lay.
These days the earth itself looks sad and senseless.
And when next day the sun mounts hot and lusty
We shake our fists and kick the ground in anger.
We have strange dreams: as that, in the early morning
We stand and watch the silver drift of stars
Turn suddenly to a flock of black-birds flying.
And once in a lifetime men from over the border,
In early summer, the season of fresh campaigns,
Come trampling down the corn, and kill our cattle.
These things we know and by good luck or guidance
Either frustrate or, if we must, endure.
We are a people; race and speech support us,
Ancestral rite and custom, roof and tree,
Our songs that tell of our triumphs and disasters
(Fleeting alike), continuance of fold and hearth,

Our names and callings, work and rest and sleep,
And something that, defeated, still endures—
These things sustain us. Yet there are times
When name, identity, and our very hands,
Senselessly labouring, grow most hateful to us,
And we would gladly rid us of these burdens,
Enter our darkness through the doors of wheat
And the light veil of grass (leaving behind
Name, body, country, speech, vocation, faith)
And gather into the secrecy of the earth
Furrowed by broken ploughs lost deep in time.

We have such hours, but are drawn back again
By faces of goodness, faithful masks of sorrow,
Honesty, kindness, courage, fidelity,
The love that lasts a life's time. And the fields,
Homestead and stall and barn, springtime and autumn.
(For we can love even the wandering seasons
In their inhuman circuit.) And the dead
Who lodge in us so strangely, unremembered,
Yet in their place. For how can we reject
The long last look on the ever-dying face
Turned backward from the other side of time?
And how offend the dead and shame the living
By these despairs? And how refrain from love?
This is a difficult country, and our home.

The Mahratta Ghats

ALUN LEWIS

THE valleys crack and burn, the exhausted plains
Sink their black teeth into the horny veins
Straggling the hills' red thighs, the bleating goats
—Dry bents and bitter thistles in their throats—

Thread the loose rocks by immemorial tracks.
Dark peasants drag the sun upon their backs.

High on the ghat the new turned soil is red,
The sun has ground it to the finest red,
It lies like gold within each horny hand.
Siva has spilt his seed upon this land.

Will she who burns and withers on the plain
Leave, ere too late, her scraggy herds of pain,
The cow-dung fire and the trembling beasts,
The little wicked gods, the grinning priests,
And climb, before a thousand years have fled,
High as the eagle to her mountain bed
Whose soil is fine as flour and blood-red?

But no! She cannot move. Each arid patch
Owns the lean folk who plough and scythe and
    thatch
Its grudging yield and scratch its stubborn stones.
The small gods suck the marrow from their bones.

Who is it climbs the summit of the road?
Only the beggar bumming his dark load.
Who was it cried to see the falling star?
Only the landless soldier lost in war.

And did a thousand years go by in vain?
And does another thousand start again?

A Polished Performance

D. J. ENRIGHT

CITIZENS of the polished capital
   Sigh for the towns up country,
And their innocent simplicity.

People in the towns up country
   Applaud the unpolished innocence
Of the distant villages.

Dwellers in the distant villages
   Speak of a simple unspoilt girl,
Living alone, deep in the bush.

Deep in the bush we found her,
   Large and innocent of eye,
Among gentle gibbons and mountain ferns.

Perfect for the part, perfect,
   Except for the dropsy
Which comes from polished rice.

In the capital our film is much admired,
   Its gentle gibbons and mountain ferns,
Unspoilt, unpolished, large and innocent of eye.

In the Bazaars of Hyderabad

(To a tune of the 'Bazaars')

SAROJINI NAIDU

WHAT do you sell, O ye merchants?
 Richly your wares are displayed.
Turbans of crimson and silver,
Tunics of purple brocade,
Mirrors with panels of amber,
Daggers with handles of jade.

What do you weigh, O ye vendors?
Saffron and lentil and rice.
What do you grind, O ye maidens?
Sandalwood, henna, and spice.
What do you call, O ye pedlars?
Chessmen and ivory dice.

What do you make, O ye goldsmiths?
Wristlet and anklet and ring,
Bells for the feet of blue pigeons,
Frail as a dragon-fly's wing,
Girdles of gold for the dancers,
Scabbards of gold for the king.

What do you cry, O ye fruitmen?
Citron, pomegranate, and plum.
What do you play, O musicians?
Cithar, sarangi, and drum.
What do you chant, O magicians?
Spells for the æons to come.

What do you weave, O ye flower-girls
With tassels of azure and red?
Crowns for the brow of a bridegroom,
Chaplets to garland his bed,
Sheets of white blossoms new-gathered
To perfume the sleep of the dead.

Monsoon

DAVID WEVILL

A SNAKE emptied itself into the grass.
A lizard wriggled out of a cup of ferns.
The pebbles, quiet, but nudging to follow the dust
Downwind, struggled with consciences,
Vaulting back as the gust, passing, kinked the long grass.
Then first we heard it, the long rush and rake
Abrading, stripping the earth's back, as the rain
Trailing its millions of wires, and voiding first
The lecture hall, the library and bungalows—
All the gardens springing taut, and the tennis courts
Smudged like wrecks at sea—the downpour came,
Caving its seething wall onto our verandahs,
Submerging the whole house. And we froze,
Like water-spiders clenched in their sacs of breathing,
Crouched, dry and firm in the damp close mouth of the
    wind,
As the tropics snapped and tore at our moderate blood—

Then after an hour the ground steamed openly.
The rain, flickering northwards into the shallow hills
Left little puddles behind, rubies aflame
In the fattened grasses drinking the sunset down,
Deep, through stem and root, and into the cave of stone
Where the scorpion hungers, carrying his bruise down.

A Hong Kong House

'AND now a dove, and now a dragon-fly
  Came to the garden; sometimes as we sat
Outdoors in twilight noiseless owl and bat
Flew shadowily by.
It was no garden,—so adust, red-dry
The rock-drift soil was, no kind root or sweet
Scent-subtle flower would house there, but I own
At certain seasons, burning bright,
Full-blown,
Some trumpet-purple blooms blazed at the sun's
  huge light.'

And then? tell more.
'The handy lizard and quite nimble toad
Had courage often to explore
Our large abode.
The infant lizard whipped across the wall
To his own objects; how to slide like him
Along the upright plane and never fall,
Ascribe to Eastern whim.
The winged ants flocked to our lamp, and shed
Their petally wings, and walked and crept instead.

'The palm-tree-top soared into the golden blue
And soaring skyward drew
Its straight stem etched with many rings,
And one broad holm-like tree whose name I never knew
Was decked through all its branches with broidering
  leaves

Of pattern-loving creepers; fine warblings
And gong-notes thence were sounded at our eaves
By clever birds one very seldom spied,
Except when they, of one tree tired,
Into another new-desired,
Over the lawn and playthings chose to glide.'

House and Land

ALLEN CURNOW

WASN'T this the site, asked the historian,
Of the original homestead?
Couldn't tell you, said the cowman;
I just live here, he said,
Working for old Miss Wilson
Since the old man's been dead.

Moping under the bluegums
The dog trailed his chain
From the privy as far as the fowlhouse
And back to the privy again,
Feeling the stagnant afternoon
Quicken with the smell of rain.

There sat old Miss Wilson,
With her pictures on the wall,
The baronet uncle, mother's side,
And one she called The Hall;
Taking tea from a silver pot
For fear the house might fall.

She's all of eighty said the cowman,
Down at the milking-shed.

I'm leaving here next winter.
Too bloody quiet, he said.

The spirit of exile, wrote the historian,
Is strong in the people still.

He reminds me rather, said Miss Wilson,
Of Harriet's youngest, Will.

The cowman, home from the shed, went
    drinking
With the rabbiter home from the hill.

The sensitive nor'west afternoon
Collapsed, and the rain came;
The dog crept into his barrel
Looking lost and lame.
But you can't attribute to either
Awareness of what great gloom
Stands in a land of settlers
With never a soul at home.

South

EDWARD BRAITHWAITE

TODAY I recapture the islands'
    Bright beaches: blue mist from the ocean
Rolling into the fishermen's houses.
By those shores I was born: sound of the sea
Came in at my window, life heaved and breathed in
    me then
With the strength of that turbulent soil.

Since then I have travelled: moved far from the beaches:
Sojourned in stoniest cities, walking the lands of the north

In sharp slanting sleet and the hail;
Crossed countless saltless savannahs and come
To this house in the forest where the shadows oppress me
And the only water is rain and the tepid taste of the river.

We who are born of the ocean can never seek solace
In rivers: their flowing runs on like our longing,
Reproves us our lack of endeavour and purpose,
Shows that our striving will founder on that.
We resent them this wisdom, their freedom: passing us
Toiling, waiting and watching their cunning declension
    down to the sea.

But today I would join you, travelling river,
Borne down the years of your patientest flowing,
Past pains that would wreck us, sorrows arrest us,
Hatred that washes us up on the flats;
And moving on through the plains that receive us,
Processioned in tumult, come to the sea.

Bright waves splash up from the rocks to refresh us
Blue sea-shells shift in their wake
And there is the thatch of the fishermen's houses, the
    path
Made of pebbles; and look:
Small urchins, combing the beaches,
Look up from their traps and call to us:

A starfish lies in its pool.
The fisherman, hawking the surf on this side
Of the reef, stands up in his boat
And halloos us: they remember me just as I left them.
And gulls, white sails slanted seaward,
Fly into the limitless morning before them.

Night falls and the vision is ended.
The drone of the groaners is ended.
Frogs croak and fireflies shimmer like stars
And shadows are crossing the stars

As I turn down the slope from the murmuring river:
An old dreamer, remembering summer.

As John to Patmos

DEREK WALCOTT

AS John to Patmos, among the rocks and the blue, live air, hounded
His heart to peace, as here surrounded
By the strewn-silver on waves, the wood's crude hair, the
rounded
Breasts of the milky bays, palms, flocks, the green and dead

Leaves, the sun's brass coin on my cheek, where
Canoes brace the sun's strength, as John, in that bleak air,
So am I welcomed richer by these blue scapes, Greek there,
So I shall voyage no more from home; may I speak here.

This island is heaven—away from the dustblown blood of cities;
See the curve of bay, watch the straggling flower, pretty is
The wing'd sound of trees, the sparse-powdered sky, when lit is
The night. For beauty has surrounded
Its black children, and freed them of homeless ditties.

As John to Patmos, in each love-leaping air,
O slave, soldier, worker under red trees sleeping, hear
What I swear now, as John did:
To praise lovelong, the living and the brown dead.

Themes

WHAT shall we sing? sings Harry.

Sing truthful men? Where shall we find
The man who cares to speak his mind:
Truth's out of uniform, sings Harry,
That's her offence
Where lunacy parades as commonsense.

Of lovers then? A sorry myth
To tickle tradesmen's palates with.
Production falls, wise men can prove,
When factory girls dream dreams of love.

Sing of our leaders? Like a pall
Proficiency descends on all
Pontific nobodies who make
Some high pronouncement every week.

Of poets then? How rarely they
Are more than summer shadow-play.
Like canvassers from door to door
The poets go, and gain no ear.

Sing of the fighters? Brave-of-Heart
Soon learns to play the coward's part,
And calls it, breaking solemn pacts,
Fair Compromise or Facing Facts.

Where all around us ancient ills
Devour like blackberry the hills

On every product of the time
Let fall a poisoned rain of rhyme,
                    sings Harry;
But praise St Francis feeding crumbs
Into the empty mouths of guns.

What shall we sing? sings Harry.

Sing all things sweet or harsh upon
These islands in the Pacific sun,
The mountains whitened endlessly
And the white horses of the winter sea,
                    sings Harry.

The Wrong Road

C. DAY LEWIS

THERE was no precise point at which to say
'I am on the wrong road.' So well he knew
Where he wanted to go, he had walked in a dream
Never dreaming he could lose his way.
Besides, for such travellers it's all but true
That up to a point any road will do
As well as another—so why not walk
Straight on? The trouble is, *after* this point
There's no turning back, not even a fork;
And you never can see that point until
After you have passed it. And when you know
For certain you are lost, there's nothing to do
But go on walking your road, although
You walk in a nightmare now, not a dream.

But are there no danger-signs? Couldn't he see
Something strange about the landscape to show
That he was near where he should not be?
Rather the opposite—perhaps the view

Gave him a too familiar look
And made him feel at home where he had no right
Of way. But when you have gone so far,
A landscape says less than it used to do
And nothing seems very strange. He might
Have noticed how, mile after mile, this road
Made easier walking—noticed a lack
Of grit and gradient; *there* was a clue.
Ah yes, if only he had listened to his feet!
But, as I told you, he walked in a dream.

You can argue it thus or thus: either the road
Changed gradually under his feet and became
A wrong road, or else it was he who changed
And put the road wrong. We'd hesitate to blame
The traveller for a highway's going askew:
Yet possibly he and it become one
At a certain stage, like means and ends.
For this lost traveller, all depends
On how real the road is to him—not as a mode
Of advancement or exercise—rather, as grain
To timber, intrinsic-real.
                    He can but pursue
His course and believe that, granting the road
Was right at the start, it will see him through
Their errors and turn into the right road again.

The Survivors

R. S. THOMAS

I NEVER told you this.
He told me about it often;
Seven days in an open boat—burned out,
No time to get food:

Biscuits and water and the unwanted sun,
With only the oars' wing-beats for motion,
Labouring heavily towards land
That existed on a remembered chart,
Never on the horizon
Seven miles from the boat's bow.

After two days song dried on their lips;
After four days speech.
On the fifth cracks began to appear
In the faces' masks; salt scorched them.
They began to think about death,
Each man to himself, feeding it
On what the rest could not conceal.
The sea was as empty as the sky,
A vast disc under a dome
Of the same vastness, perilously blue.

But on the sixth day towards evening
A bird passed. No one slept that night;
The boat had become an ear
Straining for the desired thunder
Of the wrecked waves. It was dawn when it came,
Ominous as the big guns
Of enemy shores. The men cheered it.
From the swell's rise one of them saw the ruins
Of all that sea, where a lean horseman
Rode towards them and with a rope
Galloped them up on to the curt sand.

The Dancing Seal

WHEN we were building Skua Light—
The first men who had lived a night
Upon that deep-sea Isle,
As soon as chisel touched the stone
The friendly seals would come ashore
And sit and watch us all the while,
As if they'd not seen men before,
And so, poor beasts, had never known
Men had the heart to do them harm.
They'd little cause to feel alarm
With us, for we were glad to find
Some friendliness in that strange sea,
Only too pleased to let them be
And sit as long as they'd a mind
To watch us, for their eyes were kind—
Like women's eyes it seemed to me.
So hour on hour they sat: I think
They liked to hear the chisels' clink,
And when the boy sang loud and clear
They scrambled closer in to hear,
And if he whistled sweet and shrill
The queer beasts shuffled nearer still,
But every sleek and shiny skin
Was mad to hear his violin.

When, work all over for the day,
He'd take his fiddle down and play
His merry tunes beside the sea,
Their eyes grew brighter and more bright

And burned and twinkled merrily;
And as I watched them one still night
And saw their eager sparkling eyes,
I felt those lovely seals would rise,
Some shiny night ere he could know,
And dance after him heel and toe
Unto the fiddle's heady tune.

And at the rising of the moon,
Half-daft, I took my stand before
A young seal lying on the shore
And called on her to dance with me:
And it seemed hardly strange when she
Stood up before me suddenly
And shed her black and sheeny skin
And smiled, all eager to begin . . .
And I was dancing heel and toe
With a young maiden white as snow
Unto a crazy violin.

We danced beneath the dancing moon
All night beside the dancing sea
With tripping toes and skipping heels,
And all about us friendly seals
Like Christian folk were dancing reels
Unto the fiddle's endless tune
That kept on spinning merrily
As though it never meant to stop;
And never once the snow-white maid
A moment stayed
To take a breath,
Though I was fit to drop;
And while those wild eyes challenged me
I knew as well as well could be
I must keep step with that young girl,
Though we should dance to death.
Then with a skirl
The fiddle broke:
The moon went out:

The sea stopped dead:
And in a twinkling all the rout
Of dancing folk had fled . . .
And in the chill bleak dawn I woke
Upon the naked rock alone.

They've brought me far from Skua Isle . . .
I laugh to think they do not know
That, as all day I chip the stone
Among my fellows here inland,
I smell the sea-wrack on the shore . . .
And see her snowy tossing hand,
And meet again her merry smile . . .
And dream I'm dancing all the while,
I'm dancing ever, heel and toe,
With a seal-maiden white as snow,
On the moonshiny island-strand
For ever and for evermore.

The Horses

EDWIN MUIR

BARELY a twelvemonth after
The seven days war that put the world to sleep,
Late in the evening the strange horses came.
By then we had made our covenant with silence,
But in the first few days it was so still
We listened to our breathing and were afraid.
On the second day
The radios failed; we turned the knobs; no answer.
On the third day a warship passed us, heading north,
Dead bodies piled on the deck. On the sixth day
A plane plunged over us into the sea. Thereafter
Nothing. The radios dumb;

And still they stand in corners of our kitchens,
And stand, perhaps, turned on, in a million rooms
All over the world. But now if they should speak,
If on a sudden they should speak again,
If on the stroke of noon a voice should speak,
We would not listen, we would not let it bring
That old bad world that swallowed its children quick
At one great gulp. We would not have it again.
Sometimes we think of the nations lying asleep,
Curled blindly in impenetrable sorrow,
And then the thought confounds us with its strangeness.

The tractors lie about our fields; at evening
They look like dank sea-monsters couched and waiting.
We leave them where they are and let them rust:
'They'll moulder away and be like other loam.'
We make our oxen drag our rusty ploughs,
Long laid aside. We have gone back
Far past our fathers' land.
                    And then, that evening
Late in the summer the strange horses came.
We heard a distant tapping on the road,
A deepening drumming; it stopped, went on again,
And at the corner changed to hollow thunder.
We saw the heads
Like a wild wave charging and were afraid.
We had sold our horses in our fathers' time
To buy new tractors. Now they were strange to us
As fabulous steeds set on an ancient shield
Or illustrations in a book of knights.
We did not dare go near them. Yet they waited,
Stubborn and shy, as if they had been sent
By an old command to find our whereabouts
And that long-lost archaic companionship.
In the first moment we had never a thought
That they were creatures to be owned and used.
Among them were some half-a-dozen colts
Dropped in some wilderness of the broken world,
Yet new as if they had come from their own Eden.

Since then they have pulled our ploughs and borne our
   loads,
But that free servitude still can pierce our hearts.
Our life is changed; their coming our beginning.

Goliath

WALTER DE LA MARE

STILL as a mountain with dark pines and sun
   He stood between the armies, and his shout
Rolled from the empyrean above the host:
'Bid any little flea ye have come forth,
And wince at death upon my finger-nail!'
He turned his large-boned face; and all his steel
Tossed into beams the lustre of the noon;
And all the shaggy horror of his locks
Rustled like locusts in a field of corn.
The meagre pupil of his shameless eye
Moved like a cormorant over a glassy sea.
He stretched his limbs, and laughed into the air,
To feel the groaning sinews of his breast,
And the long gush of his swollen arteries pause:
And, nodding, wheeled, towering in all his height.
Then, like a wind that hushes, he gazed and saw
Down, down, far down upon the untroubled green
A shepherd-boy that swung a little sling.

Goliath shut his lids to drive that mote
Which vexed the eastern azure of his eye
Out of his vision; and stared down again.
Yet stood the youth there, ruddy in the flare
Of his vast shield, nor spake, nor quailed, gazed up,
As one might scan a mountain to be scaled.
Then, as it were, a voice unearthly still
Cried in the cavern of his bristling ear,

'His name is Death!' . . . And, like the flush
That dyes Sahara to its lifeless verge,
His brow's bright brass flamed into sudden crimson;
And his great spear leapt upward, lightning-like,
Shaking a dreadful thunder in the air;
Span between earth and sky, bright as a berg
That hoards the sunlight in a myriad spires,
Crashed: and struck echo through an army's heart.

Then paused Goliath, and stared down again.
And fleet-foot Fear from rolling orbs perceived
Steadfast, unharmed, a stooping shepherd-boy
Frowning upon the target of his face.
And wrath tossed suddenly up once more his hand;
And a deep groan grieved all his strength in him.
He breathed; and, lost in dazzling darkness,
    prayed—
Besought his reins, his gloating gods, his youth:
And turned to smite what he no more could see.

Then sped the singing pebble-messenger,
The chosen of the Lord from Israel's brooks,
Fleet to its mark, and hollowed a light path
Down to the appalling Babel of his brain.
And like the smoke of dreaming Souffrière
Dust rose in cloud, spread wide, slow silted down
Softly all softly on his armour's blaze.

Journey of the Magi

T. S. ELIOT

'A COLD coming we had of it,
    Just the worst time of the year
For a journey, and such a long journey:
The ways deep and the weather sharp,

The very dead of winter.'
And the camels galled, sore-footed, refractory,
Lying down in the melting snow.
There were times we regretted
The summer palaces on slopes, the terraces,
And the silken girls bringing sherbet.
Then the camel men cursing and grumbling
And running away, and wanting their liquor and
    women,
And the night-fires going out, and the lack of
    shelters,
And the cities hostile and the towns unfriendly
And the villages dirty and charging high prices:
A hard time we had of it.
At the end we preferred to travel all night,
Sleeping in snatches,
With the voices singing in our ears, saying
That this was all folly.

Then at dawn we came down to a temperate valley,
Wet, below the snow line, smelling of vegetation;
With a running stream and a water-mill beating
    the darkness,
And three trees on the low sky,
And an old white horse galloped away in the meadow.
Then we came to a tavern with vine-leaves over the
    lintel,
Six hands at an open door dicing for pieces of silver,
And feet kicking the empty wine-skins.
But there was no information, and so we continued
And arrived at evening, not a moment too soon
Finding the place; it was (you may say) satisfactory.

All this was a long time ago, I remember,
And I would do it again, but set down
This set down
This: were we led all that way for
Birth or Death? There was a Birth, certainly,

We had evidence and no doubt. I had seen birth
    and death,
But had thought they were different; this Birth was
Hard and bitter agony for us, like Death, our death.
We returned to our places, these Kingdoms,
But no longer at ease here, in the old dispensation,
With an alien people clutching their gods.
I should be glad of another death.

The Starry Night

JOHN MASEFIELD

THAT starry night when Christ was born,
    The shepherds watched by Dead Man's Thorn;
They shared their supper with the dogs,
And watched the sparks flick from the logs
Where the coppings from the holly burned.

Then the dogs growled, and faces turned
To horsemen, coming from the hill.

A Captain called to them, 'Keep still . . .
We're riding, seeking for a sign
That human beings are divine . . .
Is there such marvel, hereabout?'

The shepherds said, 'Us don't know nowt.
We're Mr Jones's shepherd chaps.
Old Mr Jones might know, perhaps . . .
But if you've come this country road,
You've passed his house and never knowed.
There's someone in the town might know;
A mile on, keeping as you go.'

Long after all had disappeared,
More horsemen (from the woodland) neared;

And one, a King, with a dark skin,
Cried, 'Friends, are gods and men akin?
A wonder tells of this, they say.
Is it near here? Is this the way?'

'Why, no,' the shepherds said. . . . 'Perhaps.
We're Mr Jones's shepherd chaps.
Old Mr Jones would know, I wis,
But he'll be gone to bed by this.'

After the troop had passed away,
A third came (from the River way)
And cried, 'Good friends, we seek to find
Some guidance for the questing mind,
Eternity, in all this Death,
Some life out-living flesh and breath.
Can we find this, the way we ride?'

'You'd better picket down and bide,'
The shepherds said. 'And rest your bones.
We're shepherds here to Mr Jones.
When morning comes, you ask of he,
For he'd know more of that than we.
We're only shepherds here; so bide.'

'We cannot wait,' the horseman cried.
'Life cannot wait; Death cannot stay;
This midnight is our only day.
Push on, friends; shepherds all, farewell.
This living without Life is Hell.'

The clatter of the horse-hoofs failed,
Along the wood a barn-owl wailed;
The small mice rustled in the wood;
The stars burned in their multitude.

Meanwhile, within the little town,
The camping horsemen settled down;
The horses drank at stream and fed

On chaff, from nose-bags, picketed.
The men rolled blankets out, and stretched;
Black Nim their hard cheese supper fetched;
Then, after spirit from the gourd,
Each turned to sleep without a word,
But shortly roused again to curse
A some-one calling for a nurse
To help a woman in her woe.

All this was very long ago.

Prayer before Birth

LOUIS MACNEICE

I AM not yet born; O hear me.
Let not the bloodsucking bat or the rat or the stoat or the
club-footed ghoul come near me.

I am not yet born, console me.
I fear that the human race may with tall walls wall me,
with strong drugs dope me, with wise lies lure me,
on black racks rack me, in blood-baths roll me.

I am not yet born; provide me
With water to dandle me, grass to grow for me, trees to talk
to me, sky to sing to me, birds and a white light
in the back of my mind to guide me.

I am not yet born; forgive me
For the sins that in me the world shall commit, my words
when they speak me, my thoughts when they think me,
my treason engendered by traitors beyond me,
my life when they murder by means of my hands,
my death when they live me.

I am not yet born; rehearse me
In the parts I must play and the cues I must take when
   old men lecture me, bureaucrats hector me, mountains
      frown at me, lovers laugh at me, the white
         waves call me to folly and the desert calls
            me to doom and the beggar refuses
               my gift and my children curse me.

I am not yet born; O hear me,
Let not the man who is beast or who thinks he is God come
      near me.

I am not yet born; O fill me
With strength against those who would freeze my
   humanity, would dragoon me into a lethal automaton,
      would make me a cog in a machine, a thing with
         one face, a thing, and against all those
            who would dissipate my entirety, would
               blow me like thistledown hither and
                  thither or hither and thither
                     like water held in the
                        hands would spill me.
Let them not make me a stone and let them not spill me.
Otherwise kill me.

A Prayer for my Daughter

W. B. YEATS

ONCE more the storm is howling, and half hid
   Under this cradle-hood and coverlid
My child sleeps on. There is no obstacle
But Gregory's wood and one bare hill
Whereby the haystack- and roof-levelling wind,

Bred on the Atlantic, can be stayed;
And for an hour I have walked and prayed
Because of the great gloom that is in my mind.

I have walked and prayed for this young child an hour
And heard the sea-wind scream upon the tower,
And under the arches of the bridge, and scream
In the elms above the flooded stream;
Imagining in excited reverie
That the future years had come,
Dancing to a frenzied drum,
Out of the murderous innocence of the sea.

May she be granted beauty and yet not
Beauty to make a stranger's eye distraught,
Or hers before a looking-glass, for such,
Being made beautiful overmuch,
Consider beauty a sufficient end,
Lose natural kindness and maybe
The heart-revealing intimacy
That chooses right, and never find a friend.

Helen being chosen found life flat and dull
And later had much trouble from a fool,
While that great Queen, that rose out of the spray,
Being fatherless could have her way
Yet chose a bandy-leggèd smith for man.
It's certain that fine women eat
A crazy salad with their meat
Whereby the Horn of Plenty is undone.

In courtesy I'd have her chiefly learned;
Hearts are not had as a gift but hearts are earned
By those that are not entirely beautiful;
Yet many, that have played the fool
For beauty's very self, has charm made wise,
And many a poor man that has roved,
Loved and thought himself beloved,
From a glad kindness cannot take his eyes.

May she become a flourishing hidden tree
That all her thoughts may like the linnet be,
And have no business but dispensing round
Their magnanimities of sound,
Nor but in merriment begin a chase,
Nor but in merriment a quarrel.
O may she live like some green laurel
Rooted in one dear perpetual place.

My mind, because the minds that I have loved,
The sort of beauty that I have approved,
Prosper but little, has dried up of late,
Yet knows that to be choked with hate
May well be of all evil chances chief.
If there's no hatred in a mind
Assault and battery of the wind
Can never tear the linnet from the leaf.

An intellectual hatred is the worst,
So let her think opinions are accursed.
Have I not seen the loveliest woman born
Out of the mouth of Plenty's horn,
Because of her opinionated mind
Barter that horn and every good
By quiet natures understood
For an old bellows full of angry wind?

Considering that, all hatred driven hence,
The soul recovers radical innocence
And learns at last that it is self-delighting,
Self-appeasing, self-affrighting,
And that its own sweet will is Heaven's will;
She can, though every face should scowl
And every windy quarter howl
Or every bellows burst, be happy still.

And may her bridegroom bring her to a house
Where all's accustomed, ceremonious;
For arrogance and hatred are the wares

Peddled in the thoroughfares.
How but in custom and in ceremony
Are innocence and beauty born?
Ceremony's a name for the rich horn,
And custom for the spreading laurel tree.

Children's Song

R. S. THOMAS

WE live in our own world,
   A world that is too small
For you to stoop and enter
Even on hands and knees,
The adult subterfuge.
And though you probe and pry
With analytic eye,
And eavesdrop all our talk
With an amused look,
You cannot find the centre
Where we dance, where we play,
Where life is still asleep
Under the closed flower,
Under the smooth shell
Of eggs in the cupped nest
That mock the faded blue
Of your remoter heaven.

Warning to Children

ROBERT GRAVES

CHILDREN, if you dare to think
Of the greatness, rareness, muchness,
Fewness of this precious only
Endless world in which you say
You live, you think of things like this:
Blocks of slate enclosing dappled
Red and green, enclosing tawny
Yellow nets, enclosing white
And black acres of dominoes,
Where a neat brown paper parcel
Tempts you to untie the string.
In the parcel a small island,
On the island a large tree,
On the tree a husky fruit.
Strip the husk and pare the rind off:
In the kernel you will see
Blocks of slate enclosed by dappled
Red and green, enclosed by tawny
Yellow nets, enclosed by white
And black acres of dominoes,
Where the same brown paper parcel—
Children, leave the string untied!
For who dares undo the parcel
Finds himself at once inside it,
On the island, in the fruit,
Blocks of slate about his head,
Finds himself enclosed by dappled
Green and red, enclosed by yellow
Tawny nets, enclosed by black

And white acres of dominoes,
With the same brown paper parcel
Still unopened on his knees.
And, if he then should dare to think
Of the fewness, muchness, rareness,
Greatness of this endless only
Precious world in which he says
He lives—he then unties the string.

A Child Ill

JOHN BETJEMAN

OH, little body, do not die.
    The soul looks out through wide blue eyes
So questioningly into mine,
    That my tormented soul replies:
'Oh, little body, do not die.
    You hold the soul that talks to me
Although our conversation be
    As wordless as the windy sky.'

So looked my father at the last
    Right in my soul, before he died,
Though words we spoke went heedless past
    As London's traffic-roar outside.
And now the same blue eyes I see
    Look through me from a little son,
So questioningly, so searchingly
    That youthfulness and age are one.

My father looked at me and died
    Before my soul made full reply.
Lord, leave this other Light alight—
    Oh, little body, do not die.

A Drowning

MERVYN MORRIS

'SAVE lunch for Coke House, would you please?
   There's been an accident at the sea.'

At lunch with lively boys
Of other Houses, through the splash
Of noisy talk, the adult minds
Were shivering, worried weak. Later
The coffee tasted bitter and was cold.

'I hear something; bus is coming!'
Groaning, grinding up the hill.
A bubble of activity, the wide-eyed faces
Tilted, anxious, open for news.
A whisper and a hush
And 'Drowned, drowned, Marriott is drowned.'
The room sinks dead, swallowed in silent panic.
The mourning's private, solemn and intense.

The curious thirst for detail swells,
A wave of teachers rise
Like undertakers
And descend the cold stone steps.

A Tropical Childhood

EDWARD LUCIE-SMITH

IN the hot noons I heard the fusillade
  As soldiers on the range learnt how to kill,
Used my toy microscope, whose lens arrayed
  The twenty rainbows in a parrot's quill.

Or once, while I was swimming in the bay,
  The guns upon the other, seaward shore
Began a practice-shoot; the angry spray
  Fountained above the point at every roar.

Then I, in the calm water, dived to chase
  Pennies my father threw me, searched the sand
For the brown disc a yard beneath my face,
  And never tried to see beyond my hand.

That was the time when a dead grasshopper
  Devoured by ants before my captive eye
Made the sun dark, yet distant battles were
  Names in a dream, outside geography.

The Ball Poem

JOHN BERRYMAN

WHAT is the boy now, who has lost his ball,
  What, what is he to do? I saw it go
Merrily bouncing, down the street, and then
Merrily over—there it is in the water!

No use to say 'O there are other balls':
An ultimate shaking grief fixes the boy
As he stands rigid, trembling, staring down
All his young days into the harbour where
His ball went. I would not intrude on him,
A dime, another ball, is worthless. Now
He senses first responsibility
In a world of possessions. People will take balls,
Balls will be lost always, little boy,
And no one buys a ball back. Money is external.
He is learning, well behind his desperate eyes,
The epistemology of loss, how to stand up
Knowing what every man must one day know
And most know many days, how to stand up.
And gradually light returns to the street,
A whistle blows, the ball is out of sight,
Soon part of me will explore the deep and dark
Floor of the harbour. . . . I am everywhere,
I suffer and move, my mind and my heart move
With all that move me, under the water
Or whistling. I am not a little boy.

Legend

JUDITH WRIGHT

THE blacksmith's boy went out with a rifle
and a black dog running behind.
Cobwebs snatched at his feet,
rivers hindered him,
thorn-branches caught at his eyes to make him blind
and the sky turned into an unlucky opal,
but he didn't mind.
I can break branches, I can swim rivers, I can stare out any
   spider I meet
said he to his dog and his rifle.

The blacksmith's boy went over the paddocks
with his old black hat on his head.
Mountains jumped in his way,
rocks rolled down on him,
and the old crow cried, You'll soon be dead!
And the rain came down like mattocks.
But he only said
I can climb mountains, I can dodge rocks, I can shoot an old
  crow any day,
and he went on over the paddocks.

When he came to the end of the day the sun began falling.
Up came the night ready to swallow him,
like the barrel of a gun,
like an old black hat,
like a black dog hungry to follow him.
Then the pigeon, the magpie and the dove began wailing
and the grass lay down to pillow him.
His rifle broke, his hat blew away and his dog was gone
and the sun was falling.

But in front of the night the rainbow stood on the mountain,
just as his heart foretold.
He ran like a hare,
he climbed like a fox,
he caught it in his hands, the colours and the cold—
like a bar of ice, like the column of a fountain,
like a ring of gold.
The pigeon, the magpie, and the dove flew up to stare,
and the grass stood up again on the mountain.

The blacksmith's boy hung the rainbow on his shoulder
instead of his broken gun.
Lizards ran out to see,
snakes made way for him,
and the rainbow shone as brightly as the sun.
All the world said, Nobody is braver, nobody is bolder,
nobody else has done
anything to equal it. He went home as easy as could be,
with the swinging rainbow on his shoulder.

To My Mother

GEORGE BARKER

MOST near, most dear, most loved and most far,
  Under the window where I often found her
Sitting as huge as Asia, seismic with laughter,
Gin and chicken helpless in her Irish hand,
Irresistible as Rabelais, but most tender for
The lame dogs and hurt birds that surround her,—
She is a procession no one can follow after
But be like a little dog following a brass band.

She will not glance up at the bomber, or condescend
To drop her gin and scuttle to a cellar,
But lean on the mahogany table like a mountain
Whom only faith can move, and so I send
O all my faith and all my love to tell her
That she will move from mourning into morning.

For Granny
(*from Hospital*)

JOHN PEPPER CLARK

TELL me, before the ferryman's return,
  What was that stirred within your soul,
One night fifteen floods today,
When upon a dugout
Mid pilgrim lettuce on the Niger,

You with a start strained me to breast:
Did you that night in the raucous voice
Of yesterday's rain,
Tumbling down banks of reed
To feed a needless stream,
Then recognize the loud note of quarrels
And endless dark nights of intrigue
In Father's house of many wives?
Or was it wonder at those footless stars
Who in their long translucent fall
Make shallow silten floors
Beyond the pale of muddy waters
Appear more plumbless than the skies?

Brother and Sisters

JUDITH WRIGHT

THE road turned out to be a cul-de-sac;
stopped like a lost intention at the gate
and never crossed the mountains to the coast.
But they stayed on. Years grew like grass and leaves
across the half-erased and dubious track
until one day they knew the plans were lost,
the blue-print for the bridge was out of date,
and now their orchards never would be planted.
The saplings sprouted slyly; day by day
the bush moved one step nearer, wondering when.
The polished parlour grew distrait and haunted
where Millie, Lucy, John each night at ten
wound the gilt clock that leaked the year away.

The pianola—oh, listen to the mocking-bird—
wavers on Sunday and has lost a note.
The wrinkled ewes snatch pansies through the fence
and stare with shallow eyes into the garden

where Lucy shrivels waiting for a word,
and Millie's cameos loosen round her throat.
The bush comes near, the ranges grow immense.

Feeding the lambs deserted in early spring
Lucy looked up and saw the stockman's eye
telling her she was cracked and old.
                                        The wall
groans in the night and settles more awry.
O how they lie awake. Their thoughts go fluttering
from room to room like moths: 'Millie, are you awake?'
'Oh, John, I have been dreaming.' 'Lucy, do you cry?'
—meet tentative as moths. Antennae stroke a wing.
'There is nothing to be afraid of. Nothing at all.'

The Taste of the Fruit

(In memory of the poet Ingrid Jonker, who drowned herself by night at Sea Point, Cape Town, in July 1965; and of Nathaniel Nakasa, the South African writer, who died by suicide in the United States in the same month.)

WILLIAM PLOMER

WHERE a dry tide of sheep
        Ebbs between rocks
In a miasma of dust,
Where time is wool;
He is not there.

Where towers of green water
Crash, re-shaping
White contours of sand,
Velvet to a bare foot;
She is not there.

Where pride in modesty,
Grace, neatness,
Glorify the slum shack
Of one pensive woman;
He is not there.

Where one fatherly man
Waited with absolute
Understanding, undemanding
Hands full of comfort;
She is not there.

Where sour beer and thick smoke,
Lewdness and loud
Laughter half disguise
Hope dying of wounds;
He is not there.

He, who loved learning,
Nimbly stood up to
The heavyweight truth;
For long years in training
He is not there.

Where she was thought childlike
She carried the iron
Seeds of knowledge and wisdom;
Where they now flower,
She is not there.

A man with no passport,
He had leave to exile
Himself from the natural
Soil of his being,
But none to return.

She, with a passport,
Turned great eyes on Europe.
What did she return to?

She found, back home, that
She was not there.

Where meat-fed men are idling
On a deep stoep,
Voicing disapproval
Of those who have 'views';
She is not there.

Where with hands tied
Some wrestle for freedom;
Where with mouth stopped
Some ripen a loud cry;
He is not there.

Where intellectuals
Bunch together to follow
Fashions that allow for
No private exceptions;
She is not there.

Now he is free in
A state with no frontiers,
But where men are working
To undermine frontiers,
He is not there.

'My people,' in anguish
She cried, 'from me have rotted
Utterly away.' Everywhere
She felt rejected;
Now she is nowhere.

Where men waste in prison
For trying to be fruitful,
The first fruit is setting
Themselves dug for;
He will not taste it.

Her blood and his
Fed the slow, tormented
Tree that is destined
To bear what will be
Bough-bending plenty.

Let those who will savour
Ripeness and sweetness,
Let them taste and remember
Him, her and all others
Secreted in the juices.

Two Travellers

C. DAY LEWIS

ONE of us in the compartment stares
 Out of his window the whole day long
With attentive mien, as if he knows
There is hid in the journeying scene a song
To recall or compose
From snatches of vision, hints of vanishing airs.

He'll mark the couched hares
In grass whereover the lapwing reel and twist:
He notes how the shockheaded sunflowers climb
Like boys on the wire by the railway line;
And for him those morning rivers are love-in-a-mist,
And the chimneystacks prayers.

The other is plainly a man of affairs,
A seasoned commuter. His looks assert,
As he opens a brief-case intent on perusing
Facts and figures, he'd never divert
With profitless musing
The longest journey, or notice the dress it wears.

Little he cares
For the coloured drift of his passage: no, not a thing
Values in all that is hurrying past,
Though dimly he senses from first to last
How flaps and waves the smoke of his travelling
At the window-squares.

One is preoccupied, one just stares,
While the whale-ribbed terminus nears apace
Where passengers all must change, and under
Its arch triumphal quickly disperse.
So you may wonder,
Watching these two whom the train indifferently
    bears,

What each of them shares
With his fellow-traveller, and which is making
    the best of it,
And whether this or the other one
Will be justified when the journey's done,
And if either may carry on some reward or regret
    for it
Whither he fares.

The Man in the Bowler Hat

A. S. J. TESSIMOND

I AM the unnoticed, the unnoticeable man:
The man who sat on your right in the morning train:
The man you looked through like a windowpane:
The man who was the colour of the carriage, the colour
    of the mounting
Morning pipe smoke.

I am the man too busy with a living to live,
Too hurried and worried to see and smell and touch:
The man who is patient too long and obeys too much
And wishes too softly and seldom.

I am the man they call the nation's backbone,
Who am boneless—playable catgut, pliable clay:
The Man they label Little lest one day
I dare to grow.

I am the rails on which the moment passes,
The megaphone for many words and voices:
I am graph, diagram,
Composite face.

I am the led, the easily-fed,
The tool, the not-quite-fool
The would-be-safe-and-sound,
The uncomplaining, bound,
The dust fine-ground,
Stone-for-a-statue waveworn pebble-round.

Telephone Conversation

WOLE SOYINKA

THE price seemed reasonable, location
Indifferent. The landlady swore she lived
Off premises. Nothing remained
But self-confession. 'Madam,' I warned,
'I hate a wasted journey—I am African.'
Silence. Silenced transmission of
Pressurized good-breeding. Voice, when it came,
Lipstick coated, long gold-rolled
Cigarette-holder pipped. Caught I was, foully.

'HOW DARK?' . . . I had not misheard. . . . 'ARE YOU
  LIGHT
OR VERY DARK?' Button B. Button A. Stench
Of rancid breath of public hide-and-speak.
Red booth. Red pillar-box. Red double-tiered
Omnibus squelching tar. It *was* real! Shamed
By ill-mannered silence, surrender
Pushed dumbfounded to beg simplification.
Considerate she was, varying the emphasis—
'ARE YOU DARK? OR VERY LIGHT?' Revelation came.
'You mean—like plain or milk chocolate?'
Her assent was clinical, crushing in its light
Impersonality. Rapidly, wave-length adjusted,
I chose. 'West African sepia'—and as afterthought,
'Down in my passport.' Silence for spectroscopic
Flight of fancy, till truthfulness clanged her accent
Hard on the mouthpiece. 'WHAT'S THAT?' conceding
'DON'T KNOW WHAT THAT IS.' 'Like brunette.'
'THAT'S DARK, ISN'T IT?' 'Not altogether.
Facially, I am brunette, but madam, you should see
The rest of me. Palm of my hand, soles of my feet
Are a peroxide blonde. Friction, caused—
Foolishly madam—by sitting down, has turned
My bottom raven black—One moment madam!'—
  sensing
Her receiver rearing on the thunderclap
About my ears—'Madam,' I pleaded, 'wouldn't you
  rather
See for yourself?'

This Landscape, These People

ZULFIKAR GHOSE

I

MY eighth spring in England I walk among
    The silver birches of Putney Heath,
Stepping over twigs and stones: being stranger,
I see but do not touch: only the earth
Permits an attachment. I do not wish
To be seen, and move, eyes at my sides, like a fish.

And do they notice me, I wonder, these
    Englishmen strolling with stiff country strides?
    I lean against a tree, my eyes are knots
    In its bark, my skin the wrinkles in its sides.
    I leap hedges, duck under chestnut boughs,
And through the black clay let my swift heels trail like
        ploughs.

A child at a museum, England for me
    Is an exhibit within a glass case.
    The country, like an antique chair, has a rope
    Across it. I may not sit, only pace
    Its frontiers. I slip through ponds, jump ditches,
Through galleries of ferns see England in pictures.

2

My seventeen years in India, I swam
    Along the silver beaches of Bombay,
    Pulled coconuts from the sky and tramped
    Red horizons with the swagger and sway
    Of Romantic youth; with the impudence
Of a native tongue, I cried for independence.

A troupe came to town, marched through the villages;
   Began with two tight-rope walkers, eyes gay
   And bamboos and rope on their bare shoulders;
   A snake-charmer joined them, beard long and grey,
   Baskets of cobras on his turbaned head;
Through villages marched: children, beating on drums, led

Them from village to village, and jugglers
   Joined them and swallowers of swords, eaters
   Of fire brandishing flames through the thick air,
   Jesters with tongues obscene as crows', creatures
   Of the earth: stray dogs, lean jackals, a cow;
Stamping, shouting, entertaining, making a row

From village to village they marched to town:
   Conjurers to bake bread out of earth, poets
   To recite epics at night. The troupe, grown
   Into a nation, halted, squirmed: the sets
   For its act, though improvised, were re-cast
From the frames of an antique, slow-moving, dead past.

India halted: as suddenly as a dog,
   Barking, hangs out his tongue, stifles his cry.
   An epic turned into a monologue
   Of death. The rope lay stiff across the country;
   All fires were eaten, swallowed all the swords;
The horizons paled, then thickened, blackened with
     crows.

Born to this continent, all was mine
   To pluck and taste: pomegranates to purple
   My tongue and chillies to burn my mouth. Stones
   Were there to kick. This landscape, these people—
   Bound by the rope and consumed by their fire.
Born here, among these people, I was stranger.

3

This landscape, these people! Silver birches
   With polished trunks chalked around a chestnut.

All is fall-of-night still. No thrush reaches
Into the earth for worms, nor pulls at the root
Of a crocus. Dogs have led their masters home.
I stroll, head bowed, hearing only the sound of loam

At my heel's touch. Now I am intimate
With England; we meet, secret as lovers.
I pluck leaves and speak into the air's mouth;
As a woman's hair, I deck with flowers
The willow's branches; I sit by the pond,
My eyes are stars in its stillness; as with a wand,

I stir the water with a finger until
It tosses waves, until countries appear
From its dark bed: the road from Putney Hill
Runs across oceans into the harbour
Of Bombay. To this country I have come.
Stranger or an inhabitant, this is my home.

Time Eating

KEITH DOUGLAS

RAVENOUS Time has flowers for his food
in Autumn, yet can cleverly make good
each petal: devours animals and men,
but for ten dead he can create ten.

If you enquire how secretly you've come
to mansize from the smallness of a stone
it will appear his effort made you rise
so gradually to your proper size.

But as he makes he eats; the very part
where he began, even the elusive heart
Time's ruminative tongue will wash
and slow juice masticate all flesh.

That volatile huge intestine holds
material and abstract in its folds:
thought and ambition melt and even the world
will alter, in that catholic belly curled.

But Time, who ate my love, you cannot make
such another; you who can remake
the lizard's tail and the bright snakeskin
cannot, cannot. That you gobbled in
too quick, and though you brought me from a boy
you can make no more of me, only destroy.

One Hard Look

ROBERT GRAVES

SMALL gnats that fly
In hot July
And lodge in sleeping ears
Can rouse therein
A trumpet's din
With Day of Judgement fears.

Small mice at night
Can wake more fright
Than lions at midday;
A straw will crack
The camel's back—
There is no easier way.

One smile relieves
A heart that grieves
Though deadly sad it be,
And one hard look
Can close the book
That lovers love to see.

Ask No Man

PETER CHAMPKIN

ASK no man the question, for how
   Can man reply?
What is the reason that we are
Together, you and I?

Ask not why the world is, for who
Is wise to know?
Purpose and time are only words
In spaces where we go.

Being is reason, lovers know.
They understand
How all the universe can be
In another's hand.

Home

EDWARD THOMAS

OFTEN I had gone this way before:
   But now it seemed I never could be
And never had been anywhere else;
'Twas home; one nationality
We had, I and the birds that sang,
One memory.

They welcomed me. I had come back
That eve somehow from somewhere far:
The April mist, the chill, the calm,
Meant the same thing familiar
And pleasant to us, and strange too,
Yet with no bar.

The thrush on the oaktop in the lane
Sang his last song, or last but one;
And as he ended, on the elm
Another had but just begun
His last; they knew no more than I
The day was done.

Then past his dark white cottage front
A labourer went along, his tread
Slow, half with weariness, half with ease;
And through the silence, from his shed
The sound of sawing rounded all
That silence said.

The Troops

SIEGFRIED SASSOON

DIM, gradual thinning of the shapeless gloom
Shudders to drizzling daybreak that reveals
Disconsolate men who stamp their sodden boots
And turn dulled, sunken faces to the sky
Haggard and hopeless. They, who have beaten down
The stale despair of night, must now renew
Their desolation in the truce of dawn,
Murdering the livid hours that grope for peace.

Yet these, who cling to life with stubborn hands,
Can grin through storms of death and find a gap

In the clawed, cruel tangles of his defence.
They march from safety, and the bird-sung joy
Of grass-green thickets, to the land where all
Is ruin, and nothing blossoms but the sky
That hastens over them where they endure
Sad, smoking, flat horizons, reeking woods,
And foundered trench-lines volleying doom for doom.

O my brave brown companions, when your souls
Flock silently away, and the eyeless dead
Shame the wild beast of battle on the ridge,
Death will stand grieving in that field of war
Since your unvanquished hardihood is spent.
And through some mooned Valhalla there will pass
Battalions and battalions, scarred from hell;
The unreturning army that was youth;
The legions who have suffered and are dust.

Anthem for Doomed Youth

WILFRED OWEN

WHAT passing bells for these who die as cattle?
   Only the monstrous anger of the guns.
Only the stuttering rifles' rapid rattle
   Can patter out their hasty orisons.
No mockeries now for them; no prayers nor bells,
   Nor any voice of mourning save the choirs,—
The shrill, demented choirs of wailing shells;
   And bugles calling for them from sad shires.

What candles may be held to speed them all?
   Not in the hands of boys, but in their eyes
Shall shine the holy glimmers of good-byes.

The pallor of girls' brows shall be their pall;
Their flowers the tenderness of patient minds,
And each slow dusk a drawing-down of blinds.

Elegy for an Unknown Soldier

JAMES K. BAXTER

THERE was a time when I would magnify
His ending; scatter words as if I wept
Tears not my own but man's; there was a time.
But not now so. He died of a common sickness.

Nor did any new star shine
Upon that day when he came crying out
Of fleshy darkness to a world of pain,
And waxen eyelids let the daylight enter.

So felt and tasted, found earth good enough.
Later he played with stones and wondered
If there was land beyond the dark sea rim
And where the road led out of the farthest paddock.

Awkward at school, he could not master sums.
Could you expect him then to understand
The miracle and menace of his body
That grew as mushrooms grow from dusk to dawn?

He had the weight, though, for a football scrum,
And thought it fine to listen to the cheering
And drink beer with the boys, telling them tall
Stories of girls that he had never known.

So when the War came he was glad and sorry,
But soon enlisted. Then his mother cried

A little, and his father boasted how
He'd let him go, though needed for the farm.

Likely in Egypt he would find out something
About himself, if flies and drunkenness
And deadly heat could tell him much—until
In his first battle a shell splinter caught him.

So crown him with memorial bronze among
The older dead, child of a mountainous island.
Wings of a tarnished victory shadow him
Who born of silence has burned back to silence.

Antiquities

SIEGFRIED SASSOON

ENORMOUS aqueducts have had their day,
  And moles make mounds where marshals camped
  and clashed.
On stones where awe-struck emperors knelt to pray
The tourist gapes with guide-book, unabashed.
Historian Time, who in his 'Life of Man'
Records the whole, himself is much unread:
The breath must go from beauty, and the span
Of Lethe bleaken over all the dead.

Only the shattered arch remains to tell
Humanity its transience and to be
Life-work for archaeologists who spell
The carven hieroglyphics of Chaldee.
And where the toiling town once seethed in smoke
There'll drop, through quiet, one acorn from an oak.

In the Swamp Now

HARLEY MATTHEWS

THEY are surveying the swamp now, the surveyors,
 Mapping its shores to minute and degree,
Reckoning its expanse by link and chain.
Each motion puzzles a reflective tree,
Troubles the cloud-deeps.
                              You are right, blue crane.

Flap up, and off, and find
Among some she-oaks standing more securely
Yourself there beneath you again,
Oh, do not look behind.
That sky out there, the trees here, they will drain
Them altogether into a nowhere surely.

Go, it will all go: The ducks, that man
Wading towards them with a bush, his gun's
Report, the boy whip-cracking home the cows,
The women cooeeing them across the rise,
With none to remember it was that way once.
There is a plan
Drawn with straight-edge and square,
Decreed by a brain somewhere.
Not one inch it allows
For earth's designs or water's fantasies.

And songs? Its alphabet could never spell
One syllable
Of the frogs' poem at midnight, or the paean
Of silence after. Instead

Will rise masses and crashes of steel and stone
Shaped to one end, all else inhibited.
The grass that might persist, come drought, come rain,
Must grow precise. Trees, houses all conform,
Men too must find a norm,
To become man,
The individual perish, save the one
Who follows in the wake of the blue crane.
Yes, there'll be merriment, music, night
Vivid with light and loving, the same hope
In all hearts and minds—happiness. And oh,
And oh, the way those hearts and minds will go
To make the ideal real, and find it so
Never—On a tower a hawk will alight
One day, and men will stop,
And wonder . . . till it becomes news . . . still stare up,
And wonder if the crane had not been right.

Beleaguered Cities

F. L. LUCAS

BUILD your houses, build your houses, build your towns,
Fell the woodland, to a gutter turn the brook,
Pave the meadows, pave the meadows, pave the downs,
   Plant your bricks and mortar where the grasses shook,
   The wind-swept grasses shook.
Build, build your Babels black against the sky—
But mark yon small green glade, your stones between,
   The single spy
Of that uncounted host you have outcast;
For with their tiny pennons waving green
   They shall storm your streets at last.

Build your houses, build your houses, build your slums,
   Drive your drains where once the rabbits used to lurk,

Let there be no song there save the wind that hums
   Through the idle wires while dumb men tramp to work,
   Tramp to their idle work.
Silent the siege; none notes it; yet one day
Men from your walls shall watch the woods once more
   Close round their prey.
Build, build the ramparts of your giant-town;
Yet they shall crumble to the dust before
   The battering thistle-down.

And Death shall have No Dominion

DYLAN THOMAS

AND death shall have no dominion.
   Dead men naked they shall be one
With the man in the wind and the west moon;
When their bones are picked clean and the clean
   bones gone,
They shall have stars at elbow and foot;
Though they go mad they shall be sane,
Though they sink through the sea they shall rise again;
Though lovers be lost love shall not;
And death shall have no dominion.

And death shall have no dominion.
Under the windings of the sea
They lying long shall not die windily;
Twisting on racks when sinews give way,
Strapped to a wheel, yet they shall not break;
Faith in their hands shall snap in two,
And the unicorn evils run them through;
Split all ends up they shan't crack;
And death shall have no dominion.

And death shall have no dominion.
No more may gulls cry at their ears
Or waves break loud on the seashores;
Where blew a flower may a flower no more
Lift its head to the blows of the rain;
Though they be mad and dead as nails,
Heads of the characters hammer through daisies;
Break in the sun till the sun breaks down,
And death shall have no dominion.

Notes on the Poems

Is (p. 14)

raison d'être: a phrase from French meaning 'reason for being'.

Original Sin: a Christian doctrine which teaches that all men and women inherit a tendency to sin, deriving from the original sin of Adam, who disobeyed God and was, with Eve, driven out of the Garden of Eden. (See the Bible, Genesis iii.)

Craftsmen (p. 15)

metal founders: workers who cast metal and make objects in cast metal.

wilding: departing wildly (from the normal craft of his family).

sherds: broken pieces of pottery.

Choosing a Mast (p. 18)

rive: pull through as if to split.

oread: mountain-nymph in Greek and Latin mythology.

thews: limbs.

Muse: i.e., the Muse of poetry, who inspires poets.

thymy: adj. of *thyme*, a sweet-smelling herb; here probably the wild thyme which grows profusely in the lands of the Mediterranean.

fluvial: as of a river and its currents.

rill: a small stream.

naiad: water-nymph in Greek and Latin mythology.

azure: the blue (of the sky).

hexameters: long metrical lines (in poetry) each consisting of six feet, here used metaphorically of the long rolling waves on a seashore.

Pelion: a mountain in East Thessaly, Greece, famous in Greek mythology.

Provence: the southern part of France, edging the Mediterranean between the Alps and the Pyrenees, one of the earliest provinces of the Romans.

dryad: tree-nymph in Greek and Latin mythology.

mistral: a violent wind from the north-east which from time to time blows across the southern part of France, especially down the valley of the river Rhône.

Tartar horsemen: horsemen from the steppes of Central Asia, especially the savage warrior horsemen who overran much of Asia and eastern Europe under Genghiz Khan in the thirteenth century A.D.

fillies: young female horses.

To Walk on Hills (p. 20)

shires: counties, divisions of the country.

buzzard: bird of the falcon type, which attacks small birds and animals, and can hover in the air above its prey (hence its 'cruel poise').

plover: a type of bird that nests on the marshes and moors in England. When its nest is approached it flies away with worried cries (hence its 'misery').

Birds (p. 22)

kestrel: a type of hawk, a bird of prey.

The Exposed Nest (p. 23)

cutter-bar: the horizontal bar which contains the blades of a grass-cutting or reaping machine.

champing: biting energetically. The blades of a reaping machine are saw-like, with sharp teeth, and these move backwards and forwards rapidly to cut the crop.

The Gull (p. 25)

Attic: originally, belonging to Attica, or its capital Athens, in ancient Greece. Because Attica produced some of the finest and purest works of ancient Greek art, Attic is now often used as an adjective to denote simple purity and grace of style.

Tree Party (p. 26)

Your health: a phrase by which people 'drink the health' of others.

Willow: a tree from which cricket bats are made.

hang my harp on you: An English folksong has the lines:

> And I'll hang my harp on a weeping willow tree
> And may all the world go well with thee.

A weeping willow is a type of willow with drooping branches.

Oak: an English tree which produces hard, enduring wood. English war-ships were made of oak until they were replaced in the nineteenth century by iron ships, which were called 'ironclads' (literally 'clothed (clad) in iron').

Blackthorn: a small blossoming tree with thorns, from which sticks for walking and fighting with were commonly made.

toddy: intoxicating drink made in India and other tropical countries by tapping a certain kind of palm-tree and fermenting the juice thus obtained.

Pine: the tree from whose tall straight trunk the masts of sailing ships are often made. (See *Choosing a Mast*, p. 18).

crow's nest: the little platform high up on the mast of a large sailing ship in which stood the 'look-out', the sailor appointed to watch for land, rocks, strange ships approaching, etc.

Elm: a big spreading tree which grows to a great age, very common in the English countryside, and often used by poets in their evocations of the English rural scene. See especially here Tennyson's lines from *The Princess*:

> The moan of doves in immemorial elms,
> And murmuring of innumerable bees.

The elm is, however, subject to a tree disease which causes it to rot away inwardly, so that large branches may break off and fall, especially in a high wind (hence 'the fault in you' which 'big winds may discover').

Hazel: a small bushlike tree upon which nuts grow, gathered by country people in the autumn in England.

Hallowe'en: the 31st October, the day before All Saints' Day. The evening of Hallowe'en was traditionally celebrated with feasting and games, in which nuts and apples featured prominently. On the night of Hallowe'en ghosts were believed to walk the earth until midnight, when the advent of All Saints' Day sent them back to their resting places. The third line is an echo of *Macbeth*, V. i. 42–44.

Holly: an evergreen bush or tree with dark green spiked leaves and small red berries. Used for decoration at Christmas, holly berries were traditionally considered to symbolize the blood of Jesus, shed at the Crucifixion.

snake in you: a reference to the serpent who tempted Eve to eat the apple in the Garden of Eden; thus giving rise to a superstition that apple trees may contain snakes.

Redwood: a very tall tree of the *sequoia* species which grows in North America. The width of trunk of some redwood trees exceeds that of any other trees.

Banyan: the Indian fig-tree, whose branches drop shoots to the ground, which then take root and help to support their parent branches. By this means the banyan-tree often spreads over a great deal of ground and appears to have many trunks.

Bo-tree: an Indian tree (the pipal), closely related to the banyan, under which Gautama Buddha, the founder of Buddhism, achieved spiritual enlightenment.

Yew: a dark evergreen tree which in England is often planted in grave-yards, and is thus associated with death and burial.

postdate: put on a cheque a date in the future so that it cannot be cashed until that time arrives.

The Dead Crab (p. 30)

cote-armure: an old form of 'coat-armour', body armour or body-protecting shield worn by medieval knights.

Baby Tortoise (p. 31)

wimple: hood or veil folded round the neck or face.

Ulysses: bold adventurer. Ulysses is the Latin name of Odysseus, the hero of Homer's *Odyssey*, which tells the story of his wanderings after the Fall of Troy.

Buon viaggio: Italian for 'pleasant journey', used when saying goodbye to someone going on a journey.

Titan: one of the race of giants who, according to Greek mythology, carried on a long and fierce struggle against the gods of Olympus.

preponderate: heavy, weighty.

stoic: indifferent to pleasure or pain.

Elephant (p. 34)

krants: cliff, wall of rock (an *Afrikaans* word).

pterodactyl: an extinct prehistoric flying reptile.

Behemoth: a biblical word, derived from the Hebrew language, meaning a huge animal.

trigger-fingered: with fingers ready on the trigger (of a gun)—*i.e.*, ready to shoot at anything.

Stanley meets Mutesa (p. 36)

Henry Morton Stanley (1841–1904), journalist and explorer, became world-famous by discovering David Livingstone in 1871 on the shores of Lake Tanganyika. In 1887 he set off from the Congo towards the Nyanza area of what is now Kenya. On this journey, which took many months, he and his train of African carriers suffered great hardships, half of them dying on the way of fever and exhaustion. During this journey he made an agreement with Mutesa, the ruler of Buganda, one of a series of agreements which led to the foundation of the British East African Protectorate. There is an echo in the movement of this poem which is reminiscent, perhaps ironically, of T. S. Eliot's *Journey of the Magi* (p. 61).

Masai: a tribe of pastoral warriors who herded cattle and raided across a vast area of East Africa in what is now Kenya and Tanzania.

Nile and Nyanza: the river Nile rises in Lake Victoria in Nyanza not many miles distant from the place where Mutesa had his palace.

The Difficult Land (p. 41)

The poet may be referring to the Orkneys, in which he spent his childhood, or, more probably, to Scotland. The poem can apply to any land where it is difficult to wrest a living from the soil. The poet paints a picture of a nation without hope, yet brave and enduring. He finds nobility in their perseverance through defeat, poverty, and frustration.

The Mahratta Ghats (p. 42)

The Mahratta Ghats are a range of hills on the western side of India, east and south of Bombay, often called the Western Ghats. The writer of this poem went to India as a soldier in the Second World War and died there in the Burma campaign in 1944.

bents: stiff moorland grass.

Siva: the Hindu deity of creation and destruction.

bumming: wandering beggar-like with (his load).

A Polished Performance (p. 44)

gibbon: a type of long-armed ape.

for the part: for playing the rôle 'of a simple unspoilt girl'; also for the 'part' in the film referred to in the last verse.

dropsy: a disease which causes parts of the body to swell.

polished rice: rice with the husks removed. Because the husk of rice contains some essential foods, a diet of polished rice is inadequate for health and can cause disease, like dropsy, resulting from diet deficiencies. (The poet is here playing with the double meaning of 'polished': one as in 'polished rice' and the other as in 'polished' meaning 'sophisticated, cultured, with good manners, etc.' This emphasizes the irony of the poem.)

In the Bazaars of Hyderabad (p. 45)

Hyderabad: the town in India, formerly capital of the Muslim state of Hyderabad, in which Sarojini Naidu was born and brought up, though her family were Bengali.

brocade: woven material richly ornamented with designs in raised gold or silver thread.

vendors: salesmen.

sandalwood: a scented wood used in India, when ground and made into a paste, for anointing the body and as perfume.

henna: a reddish substance made from a plant used in India and elsewhere for colouring women's finger nails, etc.

Citron: a pale yellow fruit like a lemon but larger and less acid in flavour.

Cithar, sarangi: two stringed instruments of classical Indian music.

æons: ages.

Chaplets: wreaths (of flowers, etc.) for the head.

Monsoon (p. 46)

Monsoon: the rainy season in southern Asia brought by south-west winds.

abrading: harshly rubbing away.

scorpion hungers: scorpions hide in cracks and crevices of stone and earth during the dry season, and are able to endure hunger for very long periods.

A Hong Kong House (p. 47)

rock-drift soil: soil created by the slow powdering movement ('drift') of rocks.

whipped: moved quickly, like the flick of a whip.

holm-like: like a holm-oak, the evergreen oak-tree of Europe (*quercus ilex*), with dark leaves rather like the holly.

House and Land (p. 48)

bluegum: the *eucalyptus globulus*, a tree of Australia and New Zealand.

As John to Patmos (p. 51)

Patmos: John the Evangelist lived in old age on the Greek Island of Patmos, in the Aegean, where he wrote Revelation, the last book of the New Testament. The poet is returning to his own island in the Caribbean.

blue scapes: views (compare land*scape*, sea*scape*) which are blue because of the great expanses of sea and sky.

ditties: short, simple songs.

Themes (p. 52)

pontific: (=pontifical) characterized by the pomp of authority.

canvassers: those who go round soliciting the support and, especially, the votes of members of a community for someone who is standing for election.

St Francis: the founder of the Franciscan Order of Friars in the thirteenth century. He was a gentle and compassionate man, especially fond of animals and birds, and is often pictured feeding crumbs to hungry birds.

The Dancing Seal (p. 54)

Skua Light: the lighthouse on Skua Island, the name given to an imaginary island in the Shetland Isles to the north of Scotland. A skua is a kind of seagull that breeds in these islands.

heady: affecting the brain, intoxicating.

reels: lively dances, especially Scottish.

skirl: a shrill cry.

rout: crowd, rabble.

sea-wrack: seaweed cast ashore, or growing where it is exposed by the tide.

The Horses (p. 58)

The horses of the poet's father's farm appear here as harbingers of a new simplicity, of the lost communion with nature, of the release of natural emotion.

Last eight lines. Man has met and survived disaster. These animals, who have never known the Fall and the loss of Eden, are willing to cooperate with man and share his world of guilt and remorse.

Goliath (p. 60)

Goliath was the Philistine giant, described in the Bible, I Samuel xvii, who, after challenging the men of Israel to single combat, was killed by the young David (later to become King David) with a small stone hurled from a shepherd's sling.

empyrean: the arch of the sky, the highest heaven.

horror: this has a double meaning: the quality of exciting dread, and roughness (Latin).

locusts: insects which plague areas of Africa and Asia from time to time by migrating in swarms and eating up every green thing wherever they settle. The verb 'rustle' refers to the noise made by millions of locusts swarming over a small area.

cormorant: a large seabird, a great hunter and eater of fish, about three feet in length and black in colour.

mote: a tiny particle.

like the flush . . . Sahara: a reference to the redness of sunset or sunrise that often colours the horizon in the Sahara desert at dusk or dawn.

berg: iceberg.

reins: an old word for the loins, the lower part of the trunk of the body, at one time considered to be the centre of emotions and courage.

Babel: the city and tower described in the first book of the Bible, in Genesis xv, where the noise and confusion of many languages first arose.

Souffrière: a volcano near St Vincent in the Caribbean which erupted violently in 1812 and again in 1902, but at other times simply smoked (hence 'dreaming').

Journey of the Magi (p. 61)

The Magi were the three Wise Men who followed the Star of Bethlehem from the East to lay gifts before the infant Jesus. See the story told in the Bible, Matthew ii.

The speaker is an old man. The event of which he was a witness marked the end of an old order and the beginning of a new, but the interim is full of doubt and pain. The experience has made the old order impossible, and upset the values of traditional life, though the old king has not seen the full significance of what he witnessed at Bethlehem years before. His people continue to hold on to their gods, once his own but now alien to him. He waits impatiently for death, in the bodily sense, to release him from his spiritual discomfort and pain.

The peculiar quality of the poem lies partly in its under-statement, the matter-of-fact telling of the story contrasting with the tremendous significance of the central event of it.

lines 1–5: These lines are a poetic adaptation of a passage from a sermon by Lancelot Andrewes (1555–1626), Bishop of Winchester, in which he describes the journey of the Wise Men:

> It was no summer progress. A cold coming they had of it at this time of the year, just the worst time of the year to take a journey, and especially a long journey in. The ways deep, the weather sharp, the days short, the sun farthest off, *in solstitio brumali*, 'the very dead of winter'.

sherbet: a cooling fruit drink (the word was borrowed into English from Persian).

three trees: these are perhaps meant to suggest the three 'trees' (crosses) upon which Jesus and the two thieves were crucified on a hill outside Jerusalem.

pieces of silver: a suggestion of the soldiers who played dice for the clothing of Jesus at the foot of the cross (see the Bible, Matthew xxvi, 35); and also the thirty pieces of silver for which Judas betrayed Jesus.

set down: put down in writing; the old king can be supposed to be dictating to a scribe.

old dispensation: old order of things.

The Starry Night (p. 63)

Compare this poem with the previous poem on the same subject.

coppings: tops or heads.

nowt: nothing.

wis: guess.

picket down: tether (the horses) to a stake or peg.

bide: wait.

A Prayer for my Daughter (p. 66)

Gregory's wood: the wood belonging to Lady Gregory's house, at Coole, near Galway in Ireland. Lady Gregory was a writer and patron of the Irish literary movement, of which Yeats was a central figure. Yeats, as well as other Irish writers, often stayed with Lady Gregory at Coole, and there are many references to it in his poetry.

Helen: Helen of Troy, the divinely beautiful daughter of Zeus and Leda. In the absence of her husband, Menelaus, she was carried off to Troy by Paris, thus causing the war between the Greeks and Trojans described in Homer's *Iliad*.

a fool: i.e., Paris, who had carried her off to Troy.

that great Queen: Venus, who was born rising from the sea, according to classical mythology.

bandy-leggèd: with legs which curve outwards from one another at the knees.

smith: Hephaestus (Vulcan), the god of fire and the working of metals. Venus was unfaithful to him and became the lover of Mars, the god of war.

Horn of Plenty: a literal translation of the Latin *cornucopia*, a motif in classical art consisting of a hollow horn filled with flowers, fruit, and corn, symbolizing abundance. The reference here is to the loss of worldly abundance through women's folly. (See 'Plenty's horn' later in the poem.)

linnet: a small brown song-bird, common throughout Europe.

loveliest woman born: almost certainly a reference to Maud Gonne, an Irish nationalist with whom Yeats was in love, but who refused his hand in marriage. She inspired much of his earlier love poetry.

laurel tree: an evergreen shrub or bush whose leaves were used by the ancient Greeks and Romans as an emblem of success and distinction. Here Yeats uses it to symbolize the distinction which he believed to be inherent in a true aristocracy. The whole of this final stanza is a statement of his aristocratic ideal, for, though a staunch Irish nationalist, Yeats was not a democrat in the modern political sense.

The Ball Poem (p. 73)

dime: a silver coin of the U.S.A. and Canada worth 10 cents, about ninepence in English money.

epistemology: the philosophical study of the basis of human knowledge.

To my Mother (p. 76)

Seismic: shaken as by an earthquake.

Rabelais: François Rabelais (1495–1553), a French humanist and prose-writer whose works, especially *Pantagruel* and *Gargantua*, are full of wisdom, bawdiness, and humane satire.

Like a mountain . . . faith can move: cp. the Bible, I Corinthians xiii, 2: '. . . and though I have all faith, so that I could remove mountains . . .'

For Granny (p. 76)

It is a common belief among many of the peoples of Mid-Western Nigeria that the dead cross a river to reach the other world.

lettuce: the water-lettuce is a green cup-shaped weed that every year comes down the Niger in flood.

Brother and Sisters (p. 77)

cul-de-sac: a road which has an entry and exit at one end only, the other being closed or blocked.

pianola: a piano with mechanical means attached for playing it. Different pieces of piano music could be played by inserting different rolls of 'instructions' into the mechanism. An instrument popular before the spread of the gramophone and radio.

cameos: small stones with carved designs on them, usually set in silver and gold, and worn as ornaments by women, especially in the nineteenth and early twentieth centuries.

stockman: the man employed to look after cattle and other livestock on a farm, especially in Australia.

The Taste of the Fruit (p. 78)

This poem is an elegy for two writers of South Africa: one an Afrikaner, of the ruling race, the other an African, of the subject race. Both in their different ways were lost, and ill at ease in their country, and both committed suicide. Both, suggests the poet, are part of the growth, through trial and torment, of the better society which will one day come in South Africa.

stoep: verandah.

'*views*': liberal views, about race relations, for example, which would rouse the disapproval of those who support the existing government of South Africa.

Two Travellers (p. 81)

lapwing: a bird of the plover family which nests in the grass.

love-in-a-mist: an English name for a wild flower (the fennel) which has small yellow or white blossoms.

Telephone Conversation (p. 83)

Button B. Button A: The poet in his embarrassment stares about him at the telephone controls, at the public telephone box from which he is calling, at a pillar-box outside, and at a passing bus.

spectroscopic flight of fancy: consideration or analysis in the mind of different shades of colour.

This Landscape, These People (p. 85)

Putney Heath: Putney is a district of south-west London, and Putney Heath is adjacent to it.

chillies: hot spice made from the dried pods of the red pepper plant, much used for seasoning food in India.

Time Eating (p. 87)

make good: compensate for (by replacing something lost, stolen, or destroyed).

ruminative: engaged in 'chewing the cud', the process of *rumination*, in which cattle and other animals slowly chew and dissolve food before swallowing it.

volatile: quickly and easily changeable from one thing to another, as, *e.g.*, from liquid to gas, or in size and shape.

catholic: universal, embracing all.

The Troops (p. 90)

The troops are those of the First World War, living and fighting in trenches on the Western Front. Like Wilfred Owen (see *Anthem for Doomed Youth*), Siegfried Sassoon was an infantry officer.

Valhalla: the place in Scandinavian mythology assigned to those who die in battle, and where after death they feast with Odin, the Nordic god of war.

Anthem for Doomed Youth (p. 91)

Wilfred Owen was killed in action just before the end of the First World War. This poem laments the sacrifice of tens of thousands of young lives in the trenches of the Western Front in that War.

orisons: prayers.

pall: the cloth which covers a coffin at a funeral.

drawing-down of blinds: a reference to the custom of drawing down the window blinds of a house in which someone had just died.

Elegy for an Unknown Soldier (p. 92)

Egypt: many New Zealand soldiers fought in the North African campaigns of the Second World War.

Antiquities (p. 93)

aqueducts: artificial channels, usually made of brick or stone, for conveying water from place to place.

Lethe: in Greek mythology a river of Hades, the underworld to which people went after death. The water of Lethe produced in those who drank it forgetfulness of the past, the souls of the departed thus gaining oblivion from their earthly existence.

hieroglyphics: figures of trees, animals, etc., standing for words or sounds, and forming the elements of a species of writing found on ancient Egyptian monuments and records; hence, more generally, picture writing, symbols or enigmatic figures.

Chaldee: Babylon was the capital of the great Empire of the Chaldees, situated on the river Euphrates in what is now Iraq. The king Nebuchadnezzar took great pride in its buildings and under him it attained its greatest magnificence and splendour.

In the Swamp Now (p. 94)

minute and degree: the measures of longitude and latitude.

crane: a bird with long legs, neck, and bill which wades in marsh and shallow waters.

link and chain: a reference to the chain used by surveyors for measuring short distances.

cooeeing: calling from a distance by making the sound 'cooee', a call learnt by the Australian settlers from the aboriginal inhabitants.

straight-edge and square: draughtsman's ruler and set-square, used in drawing plans.

Beleaguered Cities (p. 95)

Babels: see note on Babel in *Goliath* (p. 60). The word is here used figuratively to refer to the noise and confusion of modern cities.

pennons: long narrow flags, such as medieval knights used on the tips of their lances.

thistle-down: the very light fluff carrying the seeds of thistle flowers.

And Death shall have No Dominion (p. 96)

unicorn evils: the unicorn is the legendary animal with a body like a horse and a single long, straight horn projecting from its forehead. The poet implies here that the evils he refers to are those which can damage and kill someone by 'running them through', piercing them as the unicorn might with its horn.

Biographical Notes

AUDEN, WYSTAN HUGH (1907). Born at York. Educated Gresham's School, Holt, and Christ Church, Oxford. Schoolmaster, and later wrote documentaries. Became naturalized American citizen, 1938. Professor of Poetry at Oxford, 1956–60. Poet, dramatist, and critic. Works include: *Poems* (1930); *The Dog beneath the Skin* (1935)—drama; *Look, Stranger* (1936); *Letters from Iceland* (1937)—with Louis MacNeice; *Collected Shorter Poems 1930–44* (1950); *The Shield of Achilles* (1955); *Homage to Clio* (1960); *About the House* (1966).

AWOONOR-WILLIAMS, GEORGE (1935). Born at Wheta, near Keta in the Togo Region of Ghana, of Sierra Leonian and Togolese descent. Educated at Achimota and the University of Ghana, where he now works in the Institute of African Studies, specializing in vernacular poetry. Edits the Ghanaian literary review, *Okyeame*. Works: *Rediscovery* (1964).

BARKER, GEORGE (1913). Born in Essex. Educated L.C.C. school in Chelsea and the Regent Street Polytechnic. Taught English Literature at Tokyo University, 1939. Writes for a living. Works include: *Poems* (1935); *Calamiterror* (1937); *Lament and Triumph* (1940); *Collected Poems* (1957); *The View from a Blind Eye* (1962).

BAXTER, JAMES KEIR (1926). Born in New Zealand. Works: *Beyond the Palisade* (1944); *Blow, Wind of Fruitfulness* (1948); *The Fallen House* (1953); *Howrah Bridge* (1961).

BERRYMAN, JOHN (1914). Born in Oklahoma, U.S.A. Educated Columbia College and Clare College, Cambridge. Has taught at Harvard and Princeton. Poet, critic and short-story writer. Works: *Poems* (1942); *The Dispossessed* (1948); *77 Dream Songs* (1964).

BETJEMAN, JOHN (1906). Born in London. Educated Marlborough and Magdalen College, Oxford. Poet and topographer. Works include: *Continual Dew* (1937); *Old Lights for New Chancels* (1940); *A Few Late Chrysanthemums* (1954); *Collected Poems* (1958); *Summoned by Bells* (1960).

BLUNDEN, EDMUND CHARLES (1896). Born at Yalding, Kent. Educated Christ's Hospital and Queen's College, Oxford. Professor of English Literature, Tokyo University, 1924–27. Fellow and Tutor in English Literature, Merton College, Oxford, 1931–44. Professor of English Literature, University of Hong Kong, 1953–64. Professor of Poetry at Oxford, 1966. Works include: *The Waggoner and Other Poems* (1920); *Undertones of War* (1928)—prose; *Collected Poems* (1930); *Poems, 1930–40* (1941); *After the Bombing* (1949); *A Hong Kong House* (1964).

BRAITHWAITE, EDWARD (1930). Born in Barbados. Educated in Barbados and at Pembroke College, Cambridge. Lecturer in History at the University of the West Indies. Has had short stories broadcast on the BBC, plays performed and published in the West Indies and Africa, and has published in various magazines.

BRETTELL, N. H. (1908). Born at Lye, Worcestershire. Educated Birmingham University. Since 1934 has taught in Southern Rhodesia. Works: *A Rhodesian Leave*; *Bronze Frieze* (1950).

CAMPBELL, ROY DUNNACHIE (1901–57). Born at Durban, Natal. Educated Durban and Natal University. Lived mostly in Spain, Portugal and France. Became a professional bull-fighter and steer-thrower. Works include: *The Flaming Terrapin* (1924); *Adamastor* (1928); *Collected Poems* (1949; 1957).

CHAMPKIN, PETER (1918). Born in Hong Kong. Educated King's School, Canterbury, and St Catharine's College, Cambridge. Taken prisoner at Dunkirk. Administrator G.C.E. Examinations, London University. Works: *In Another Room* (1959); *The Enmity of Noon* (1960); *Poems of Our Time* (1962); *For the Employed* (1966).

CLARK, JOHN PEPPER (1935). Born in the Ijaw country of the Niger Delta, Nigeria. Educated Government College, Warri, and the University College, Ibadan. Journalist since 1960. Now at Princeton on a Fellowship. Works: *Poems* (1962); *Song of a Goat* (1962)—play; *America, Their America* (1964)—prose; *Three Plays* (1965); *A Reed in the Tide* (1965).

CURNOW, ALLEN (1911). Born at Timaru, New Zealand. Educated Christchurch Boys' High School and St John's College, Auckland University. Lecturer in English, Auckland University. Works include:

Enemies (1937); *Island and Time* (1941); *At Dead Low Water* (1949); *Poems, 1949–57* (1957); *A Small Room with Large Windows* (1962).

DE LA MARE, WALTER JOHN (1873–1956). Born in Kent. Educated St Paul's Cathedral Choir School, London. Since 1908 devoted his time to literature. Works include: *Henry Brocken* (1904)— a prose romance; *Poems* (1906); *Memoirs of a Midget* (1921)—fiction; *Come Hither* (1923)—an anthology; *Collected Poems* (1942); *The Burning Glass* (1945); *The Traveller* (1946); *Winged Chariot* (1950).

DOUGLAS, KEITH (1920–44). Educated Christ's Hospital and Merton College, Oxford. Went through North African campaign. Killed near Tilly. Works: *Selected Poems* (1943); *From Alamein to Zem-Zem* (1946)—diary and poems; *Bête Noire* (1949); *Collected Works* (1966).

ELIOT, THOMAS STEARNS (1888–1965). Born at St Louis, Missouri. Educated Harvard, the Sorbonne, and Merton College, Oxford. In 1914 settled in London, where he subsequently lived, becoming a naturalized Englishman in 1927. Helped to found *The Criterion*. Awarded Nobel Prize for Literature, 1948. Works include: *Prufrock and other Observations* (1917); *Poems* (1919); *The Sacred Wood* (1920)— criticism; *The Waste Land* (1922); *Murder in the Cathedral* (1935) and *The Family Reunion* (1939)—plays; *Collected Poems* (1936); *Four Quartets* (1944).

ENRIGHT, DENNIS JOSEPH (1920). Born at Leamington. Educated Leamington College and Downing College, Cambridge. Has been an extension lecturer in English, and has lectured abroad at universities in Berlin, Egypt, Japan, and Thailand. Professor of English at Singapore. Works include: *The Laughing Hyena* (1953); *Some Men are Brothers* (1960); *Addictions* (1962); *The Old Adam* (1965).

FROST, ROBERT LEE (1874–1963). Born in San Francisco. Educated Dartmouth and Harvard University. Moved at an early age to New England. From 1911 to 1915 he lived in England. Returning to the United States, he devoted himself to poetry and teaching. Works include: *A Boy's Will* (1913); *Collected Poems* (1930).

FULLER, ROY (1912). Born at Oldham, Lancs. Educated Blackpool High School. Solicitor. Poet and novelist. Works include: *The*

Middle of a War (1942); *Epitaphs and Occasions* (1949); *The Ruined Boys* (1959)—fiction; *Collected Poems* (1962); *Buff* (1965).

GHOSE, ZULFIKAR (1935). Born at Sialkot, Pakistan. Educated Keele University. Writes book reviews and broadcasts. Poems included in *A Group Anthology* (1963); *The Loss of India* (1964).

GIBSON, WILFRID WILSON (1878–1962). Born at Hexham, Northumberland. Works include: *Stonefolds* (1907); *Collected Poems* (1926); *The Golden Room* (1928); *The Outpost* (1944).

GLOVER, DENIS (1912). Born at Dunedin, New Zealand. Educated Auckland Grammar School and Christ's College, Canterbury University. Founded Caxton Press, 1938. Tutor, Printing Department, Technical Correspondence Institute, Wellington. Works include: *Thistledown* (1935); *The Wind and the Sand, Poems, 1943–44* (1945); *Sings Harry and Other Poems* (1951); *Arawata Bill: A Sequence of Poems* (1953).

GRAVES, ROBERT (1895). Born in London. Educated Charterhouse and St John's College, Oxford. Professor of English Literature, Cairo University, 1926. Has lived in Majorca since 1947. Professor of Poetry at Oxford 1961–65. Works include: *Goodbye to All That* (1929)—autobiography; *I, Claudius* (1934)—fiction; *Collected Poems* (1938); *Poems, 1938–1945* (1946); *Collected Poems* (1959); *More Poems* (1961); *New Poems* (1962); *Man Does, Woman Is* (1964); *Love Respelt* (1965).

HESKETH, PHOEBE (1909). Educated at Cheltenham. Worked on an English northern newspaper for two years. Works: *Lean Forward, Spring* (1948); *No Time for Cowards* (1952).

HUGHES, TED (1930). Born in the West Riding of Yorkshire. Educated Mexborough Grammar School and Pembroke College, Cambridge. Works: *The Hawk in the Rain* (1957); *Lupercal* (1960); *Meet My Folks* (1961)—verse for children.

JOHNSON, GEOFFREY (1900). Born in the Black Country of the English Midlands. Educated Wolverhampton Grammar School and London University. Retired grammar-school master. Works include: *The Quest Unending.*

(1930); *Mother to Son* (1935); *The Ninth Wave* (1948); *A Man of Vision* (1958).

KAVANAGH, PATRICK (1905). Born in County Monaghan, Eire. Educated Common National School. Left school at thirteen. Has tramped all over Ireland. Works include: *Ploughman and Other Poems* (1936); *The Green Fool* (1938)—autobiography; *The Great Hunger* (1942); *Tarry Flynn* (1948)—fiction; *Come Dance with Kitty Stobling* (1960); *Collected Poems* (1963).

LARKIN, PHILIP (1922). Born at Coventry. Educated King Henry VIII School, Coventry, and St John's College, Oxford. Librarian of Hull University. Works: *The North Ship* (1945); *The Less Deceived* (1955); *The Whitsun Weddings* (1964).

LAWRENCE, DAVID HERBERT (1885–1930). Born at Eastwood, Nottinghamshire. Educated Nottingham High School and Nottingham Day Training College. Qualified as a school teacher. Travelled in Italy, Australia, and New Mexico. Novels include: *The White Peacock* (1911); *Sons and Lovers* (1913); *Women in Love* (1921). *Collected Poems* (1928); *Last Poems* (1933).

LEWIS, ALUN (1918–44). Born in a Welsh mining village. Educated University of Wales. Schoolmaster. Two years in India. Died in an accident. Works: *Raiders' Dawn* (1942); *The Last Inspection* (1943)—short stories; *Ha! Ha! Among the Trumpets* (1944).

LEWIS, CECIL DAY (1904). Born in Queen's County, Ireland. Educated Sherborne School and Wadham College, Oxford. Schoolmaster, 1927–35. Poet, novelist and critic. Writes detective novels under the pseudonym of Nicholas Blake. Professor of Poetry at Oxford, 1951–56. Works include: *Country Comet* (1928); *From Feathers to Iron* (1931); *Word over All* (1943); *Collected Poems* (1954); *Pegasus and Other Poems* (1957); *The Gate* (1962); *The Room* (1965).

LUCAS, FRANK LAURENCE (1894). Born at Hipperholme, Yorkshire. Educated Rugby and Trinity College, Cambridge. Fellow and Lecturer of King's College, Cambridge, since 1920. University Lecturer in English. Works include: *Time and Memory* (1929); *Eight Victorian Poets* (1930); *Poems* (1935); *From Many Times and Lands* (1953).

[115]

LUCIE-SMITH, EDWARD (1933). Born Kingston, Jamaica. Educated King's School, Canterbury, and Merton College, Oxford.
Copywriter in advertising agency. Writes art criticism and book
reviews and broadcasts. Works: *A Tropical Childhood* (1961); Editor
of *A Group Anthology* (1963); *Confessions* (1965).

MacNEICE, FREDERIC LOUIS (1907–63). Born in Belfast. Educated Marlborough and Merton College, Oxford. Lecturer in
Classics, Birmingham University, 1931. Lecturer in Greek, Bedford
College, London, 1936–41. Member of the staff of the BBC, engaged
in writing and producing radio plays and features, 1941–49. Director
of the British Institute at Athens, 1950. Works include: *Poems* (1935);
Letters from Iceland (1937)—with W. H. Auden; *Autumn Journal*
(1939); *The Dark Tower* (1947)—radio plays; *Collected Poems* (1949);
Solstices (1960); *The Burning Perch* (1963).

MASEFIELD, JOHN (1878). Born at Ledbury, Herefordshire. Educated King's School, Warwick, and Training Ship *Conway*. Went to
sea at an early age. Spent years in adventure by sea and land, chiefly
America, where he earned his living by doing odd jobs. Returned to
England, and devoted himself to literature—poems, plays, novels,
etc. Poet Laureate since 1930. Works include: *Salt-Water Ballads*
(1902); *The Everlasting Mercy* (1911); *Dauber* (1913); *Reynard the Fox*
(1919); *Right Royal* (1920); *Collected Poems* (1923); *Sard Harker*
(1924) and *Odtaa* (1926)—fiction; *A Tale of Troy* (1932); *Collected
Poems* (1946); *So Long to Learn* (1952)—autobiography; *The Bluebells*
(1961); *Old Raiger* (1965).

MATTHEWS, HARLEY (1889). Born at Fairfield, New South Wales.
Legal work for eight years. At Gallipoli with the Anzacs. From 1922,
devoted himself to farming, making wine, and writing poetry. Works
include: *Under the Open Sky* (1912); *Vintage* (1938); *The Breaking of
the Drought* (1940); *Patriot's Progress* (1964).

MORRIS, MERVYN (1937). Born at Kingston, Jamaica. Educated
Munro College, Jamaica, the University College of the West Indies,
and St Edmund Hall, Oxford. Schoolmaster. Poems in periodicals and
anthologies.

MORAES, DOM (1938). Father editor of *Indian Express*. Educated
Jesus College, Oxford. Lives in England. Poet and author. Works:
A Beginning (1957); *Poems* (1960); *John Nobody* (1965).

MUIR, EDWIN (1887–1959). Born in the Orkney Islands. Educated Kirkwall Burgh School. Warden of Newbattle Abbey College, 1950–1955. Poet, journalist, and translator. Works include: *First Poems* (1925); *Variations on a Time-theme* (1934); *Journeys and Places* (1937); *Collected Poems* (1952); *One Foot in Eden* (1956).

NAIDU, SAROJINI (1878–1949). Born in Hyderabad. Educated Hyderabad, King's College, London, and Girton College, Cambridge. Delivered lectures and addresses all over India on questions of social, religious, educational, and national progress. A Congress leader and a State Governor. Works include: *The Bird of Time* (1912); *The Golden Threshold*.

OKARA, GABRIEL (1921). Born in the Ijaw country of the Niger Delta, Nigeria. Educated Government College, Umuahia. Information Officer with the Eastern Regional Government at Enugu. Several of his poems have appeared in *Black Orpheus*, 1957 onwards. *The Voice* (1965)—fiction.

OWEN, WILFRED (1893–1918). Born at Oswestry. Educated Birkenhead Institute and London University. Served in the War, was awarded the M.C., and was killed in action a week before the Armistice. Works: *Poems* (1920)—with an introduction by Siegfried Sassoon; *Poems* (1933)—new edition, with notices of his life and work by Edmund Blunden.

PLOMER, WILLIAM (1903). Born at Pietersburg, Northern Transvaal. Educated Rugby. Has been a farmer and a trader, and has travelled widely. Poet, novelist, short-story writer, editor, and biographer. Works include: *Notes for Poems* (1928); *Visiting the Caves* (1936); *Double Lives* (1943)—autobiography; *Collected Poems* (1960).

REED, HENRY (1914). Born in Birmingham. Educated King Edward VI School, Birmingham, and Birmingham University. Freelance journalist and writer for broadcasting. Works: *A Map of Verona* (1946).

RUBADIRI, DAVID (1930). Born in Malawi (Nyasaland). Educated Makerere College, Kampala, Uganda, and then at King's College, Cambridge. Works in the Malawi Ministry of Education and is a teacher.

SACKVILLE-WEST, VITA (1892–1962). Born at Knole, Sevenoaks. Educated at home. Works include: *Poems of East and West* (1917); *The Land* (1926); *The Edwardians* (1930)—fiction; *Collected Poems* (1934); *The Garden* (1946).

SASSOON, SIEGFRIED LORAINE (1886). Born in London. Educated Marlborough and Clare College, Cambridge. Works include *The Old Huntsman* (1917); *War Poems* (1919); *Memoirs of a Fox-hunting Man* (1928)—autobiography; *Vigils* (1936); *Collected Poems* (1947); *Sequences* (1956).

SOYINKA, WOLE (1935). Born at Abeokuta in the Yoruba country of Western Nigeria. Educated in Ibadan at Government College and University College, then at Leeds University. Actor, musician, and poet. An editor of *Black Orpheus*. Works: *A Dance of the Forests* (1963) —a verse play; *The Interpreters* (1965)—fiction; *The Road* (1965)—a play.

TESSIMOND, ARTHUR SEYMOUR JOHN (1902–62). Born at Birkenhead, Cheshire. Educated Charterhouse and Liverpool University. Advertising copywriter since 1924. Works: *The Walls of Glass* (1934); *Voices in a Giant City* (1947).

THOMAS, DYLAN MARLAIS (1914–53). Born in Swansea. Educated Swansea Grammar School. Poet, short-story writer, script writer and broadcaster. Works include: *Eighteen Poems* (1934); *Portrait of the Artist as a Young Dog* (1940)—autobiography; *Deaths and Entrances* (1946); *Under Milk Wood* (1954)—a radio play; *Collected Poems, 1934–1952* (1952); *Adventures in the Skin Trade* (1955)—fiction.

THOMAS, PHILIP EDWARD (1878–1917). Educated St Paul's School and Lincoln College, Oxford. Killed in action at Arras, April 1917. Prose works on the English countryside. Works include: *The Woodland Life* (1897)—nature studies; *Poems* (1917); *Collected Poems* (1920); *The Childhood of Edward Thomas* (1938)—a fragment of autobiography.

THOMAS, RONALD STUART (1913). Born at Cardiff. Educated the University College of North Wales at Bangor. A clergyman. Now a vicar in Cardiganshire. Works include: *The Stones of the Fields*

(1946); *Song at the Year's Turning* (1955); *Poetry for Supper* (1958); *Tares* (1961); *The Bread of Truth* (1963).

THWAITES, MICHAEL (1915). Born in Brisbane. Rhodes Scholar at Oxford, where he won the Newdigate Prize. Lectured in English for two years at Melbourne University. Now a member of the Commonwealth Civil Service. Works: *The Jervis Bay and Other Poems* (1950).

WALCOTT, DEREK (1930). Born in St Lucia in the West Indies. Educated the University College of the West Indies. In 1957 awarded a Fellowship by the Rockefeller Foundation to study the American theatre. Works: *In a Green Night* (1962); *The Castaway* (1965).

WEVILL, DAVID (1937). Born in Japan. Educated Trinity College School, Ontario, and Caius College, Cambridge. Works: *Penguin Modern Poets* (1963); *The Birth of a Shark* (1964).

WRIGHT, JUDITH (1915). Born at Arundell, New South Wales. Educated New English Girls' School, Armidale, N.S.W., and Sydney University. Has lectured on Australian literature at various Australian universities. Now, poultry and vegetable farmer in Queensland. Works: *The Moving Image* (1946); *Woman to Man* (1949); *The Gateway* (1953); *The Two Fires* (1955); Editor of *The Oxford Book of Australian Verse*.

YEATS, WILLIAM BUTLER (1865–1939). Born at Sandymount, near Dublin. Educated Godolphin School, Hammersmith, and Erasmus Smith School, Dublin. Art student for three years, but left art for literature. The leading figure in the Irish literary renaissance. Helped to found the Abbey Theatre, Irish National Theatre (1899). Senator of the Irish Free State. Awarded the Nobel Prize for Literature, 1923. Works include: *The Wanderings of Oisin* (1889); *The Countess Cathleen* (1892)—a play; *Poems* (1895); *Plays for an Irish Theatre* (1912); *Later Poems* (1923); *The Tower* (1928); *Collected Poems* (1933); *Last Poems and Plays* (1941).

YOUNG, ANDREW (1885). Born in Elgin. Educated Royal High School, Edinburgh, and Edinburgh University. A canon of Chichester Cathedral since 1948, and Vicar of Stonegate, Sussex, since 1941. Works include: *Winter Harvest* (1933); *Collected Poems* (1936 and 1948); *Quiet as Moss* (1959).

Index of First Lines

Acknowledgments

Thanks are due to the following for kind permission to print the poems included in this Anthology:

W. H. Auden and Messrs Faber and Faber, Ltd, for poem from *Collected Shorter Poems*; George Barker and Messrs Faber and Faber, Ltd, for poem from *Collected Poems, 1930–1955*; James K. Baxter and the Oxford University Press, for poem from *Fires of No Return*; John Berryman and Messrs Faber and Faber, Ltd, for poem from *Homage to Mistress Bradstreet*; John Betjeman and Messrs John Murray, Ltd, for poem from *Collected Poems*; Edmund Blunden and Messrs A. D. Peters and Co., for poem from *A Hong Kong House*; Edward Braithwaite and Messrs William Heinemann, Ltd, for poem from *Young Commonwealth Poets, '65*; N. H. Brettell and the Oxford University Press, for poem from *A Book of South African Verse*; the Executors of Roy Campbell and Messrs The Bodley Head, Ltd, for poem from *Collected Poems*; Peter Champkin and Messrs Robert Hale, Ltd, for poem from *The Enmity of Noon*; Allen Curnow and the Oxford University Press, for poem from *A Small Room with Large Windows*; the Literary Trustees of Walter de la Mare and the Society of Authors as their representative, for poem from *Collected Poems*; Mrs Marie J. Douglas and Messrs Faber and Faber, Ltd, for poem from *Collected Poems* by the late Keith Douglas; the Executors of T. S. Eliot and Messrs Faber and Faber, Ltd, for poem from *Collected Poems*; D. J. Enright and David Higham Associates, Ltd, for poem from *Some Men are Brothers*; the Executors of Robert Frost, Messrs Jonathan Cape, Ltd, and Messrs Holt, Rinehart and Winston, Inc., for poem from *The Complete Poems of Robert Frost*; Roy Fuller and Messrs André Deutsch, Ltd, for poem from *Collected Poems*; Zulfikar Ghose and the Oxford University Press, for poem from *A Group Anthology*; Denis Glover and the Caxton Press, for poem; Michael Gibson and Messrs Macmillan and Co., Ltd, for poem from *Collected Poems, 1909–1925* by Wilfrid Gibson; Robert Graves and International Authors N.V., and Messrs Cassell and Co., Ltd, for poems from *Collected Poems, 1965*; Phoebe Hesketh and Messrs William Heinemann, Ltd, for poem from *No Time for Cowards*; Ted Hughes and Messrs Faber and Faber, Ltd, for poem from *Lupercal*; Geoffrey Johnson, for poems; Patrick Kavanagh and Messrs MacGibbon and Kee, Ltd, for poem from *Come Dance with Kitty Stobling*; Philip Larkin and Messrs Faber and Faber, Ltd, for poem from *The Whitsun Weddings*; the Estate of the late Mrs Frieda Lawrence and Messrs Laurence Pollinger, Ltd, for poem from *The Complete Poems of D. H. Lawrence*; the Executors of Alun Lewis and Messrs George Allen and Unwin, Ltd, for poem from *Ha! Ha! Among the Trumpets*; Cecil Day Lewis and Messrs Jonathan Cape, Ltd, for poems from *Collected Poems* and *Pegasus and other Poems*; F. L. Lucas and the Hogarth Press, Ltd, for poem from *Time and Memory*; Edward Lucie-Smith and the Oxford University Press, for poem from *A Tropical Childhood*; the Executors of Louis MacNeice and Messrs Faber and Faber, Ltd, for poems from *Collected Poems* and *The Burning Perch*; Dr John Masefield, O.M., and the Society of Authors, for poems from *Collected Poems* and *The Bluebells and other Poems*; Harley Matthews and Penguin Books, Ltd, for poem from *The Penguin Book of Australian Verse*; Dom Moraes and Messrs Eyre and Spottiswoode, Ltd, for poem from *Poems*; Mervyn Morris and the Editor of *The Times Literary Supplement*, for poem; the Executors of Edwin Muir and Messrs Faber and Faber, Ltd, for poems from *Collected Poems*; the Executors of Sarojini Naidu and Messrs William Heinemann, Ltd, for poem from *The Bird of Time*; Harold Owen and Messrs Chatto and Windus, Ltd, for poem from *Collected Poems* by Wilfred Owen; William Plomer and the Editor of *The Times Literary Supplement*, for poem; Henry Reed and Messrs Jonathan Cape, Ltd, for poem from *The Map of Verona*; Harold Nicolson and Messrs William Heinemann, Ltd, for poem from *Collected Poems* by the late V. Sackville-West; Siegfried Sassoon and Messrs Faber and Faber, Ltd, for poems from *Collected Poems* and *Rhymed Ruminations*; Hubert Nicholson and Messrs William Heinemann, Ltd, for poem from *Voices in a Giant City* by the late A. S. J. Tessimond; the Literary Executors of the Dylan Thomas Estate and Messrs J. M. Dent and Sons, Ltd, for poem from *Collected Poems* by Dylan Thomas; Mrs Edward Thomas and Messrs Faber and Faber, Ltd, for poem from *Collected Poems* by Edward Thomas; R. S. Thomas and Messrs Rupert Hart-Davis, Ltd, for poems from *Song at the Year's Turning* and *The Bread of Truth*; Michael Thwaites and Messrs Putnam and Co., Ltd, for poem from *The Jervis Bay and other Poems*; Derek Walcott and Messrs Jonathan Cape, Ltd, for poem from *In a Green Night*; David Wevill and Penguin Books, Ltd, for poem from *Penguin Modern Poets*; Judith Wright and Meanjin Press, Ltd, for 'Brother and Sisters', and Messrs Angus and Robertson, Ltd, for poems; M. B. Yeats and Messrs Macmillan and Co., Ltd, for poem from *The Collected Poems of W. B. Yeats*; Andrew Young and Messrs Rupert Hart-Davis, Ltd, for poem from *Collected Poems*.